O The Chimneys

Translated from the German by

MICHAEL HAMBURGER

CHRISTOPHER HOLME

RUTH and MATTHEW MEAD

MICHAEL ROLOFF

NELLY SACHS

O THE CHIMNEYS

Selected Poems, including
the verse play, ELI

FARRAR, STRAUS AND GIROUX · New York

Library of Congress catalog card number: 67–27518

Printed in the United States of America
by American Book–Stratford Press, Inc.
Published simultaneously in Canada
by Ambassador Books, Ltd., Rexdale, Ontario

FIRST PRINTING, *1967*

Designed by Herb Johnson

Selected from Fahrt ins Staublose © *Suhrkamp Verlag, Frankfurt am Main, 1961;* Zeichen im Sand © *Suhrkamp Verlag, Frankfurt am Main 1962; and* Späte Gedichte, *Suhrkamp Verlag, Frankfurt am Main 1965.*

Grateful acknowledgment is made to the editors of Harper's *Magazine,* Mademoiselle, *and* Book Week, *in whose pages some of the poems have appeared, and to the editors of* The New Yorker, *in whose pages the following poems have been published: "When day grows empty," "Agony," "Chorus of the Unborn," "Earth, old man of the planets," "And we who move," "Landscape of screams," "How many drowned ages," "The sleepwalker," "You in the night," and "Vainly."*

Introduction

BY *Hans Magnus Enzensberger*

The *oeuvre* of Nelly Sachs is great and mysterious, two attributes that literary criticism has few occasions to apply to poetry these days. They are archaic attributes; let us define their meaning. Greatness has nothing to do with talent, and little to do with the bourgeois concept of genius that makes the creator unique among men and seeks to place him in the realm of the incomparable. The poet as superman, intellectual prince, Olympian, Titan belonged to the repertoire of the nineteenth century and passed away with it. Greatness has a more ancient heritage; it can be unobtrusive; it can neither be earned nor rewarded, least of all with the prizes our society is in a position to bestow: with success or "name." Greatness remains alien in the world, and the world cannot make better sense of it than in terms of fame, which itself is an archaic and almost obsolete response. Fame, quiet fame, has come to Nelly Sachs in recent years, late and unexpectedly. But as much as greatness is a mark of the person and not only of the work, one hesitates to claim greatness exclusively for her: on the contrary, her greatness is representative. It stands for others and their cause; out of her speaks more than herself. That cause remains indeterminate and nameless, however. And this indeterminateness has something to do with the mystery of her work, which is always, in Goethe's words, a manifest secret and not comparable to mystification or murky profundity.

The poems of Nelly Sachs are of this character: hard, but transparent. They do not dissolve in the weak solution of interpretations. Nor, at first, are they easy to read. One is in the habit of saying, usually as a reproach, about all of modern poetry that it is difficult, as though this were a foregone conclusion; as if it were up to the authors to express themselves a little more obligingly. On this account it is often forgotten where the difficulty really lies. With Nelly Sachs the difficulty is never of a technical nature; she neither means to be calculating nor to shock; her poetry is neither a secret code nor a picture puzzle: what we are dealing with here are enigmas that do not add up when they are solved, but still retain an enigmatic aspect—and that aspect is what matters. Here interpretation can easily be overeager. The work demands of the reader not cleverness so much as humility: the work does not want to be made concrete or be transformed, but experienced, patiently and with exactness. Therefore, it should not be said what the work means; at most we can allow ourselves allusions, suggestions to show the reader the way—one possible way.

Gottfried Benn used to speak about his poems as though they could be understood one at a time, each one by itself—valuable "creations" which, if he was lucky, "were fit to survive," detached from any context and sufficient unto themselves. This is not so with Nelly Sachs's poetry, which is inconceivable as a series of individual artifacts. Since the appearance in 1946 of her first collection of poetry, *In the Habitations of Death,* she has been writing fundamentally a single book. The precedence of the whole over the individual in her work is not a formal characteristic; it does not express itself in an underlying structural law, in the composition as a cyclical or epic structure; it is more deeply rooted. This idea of *the book* that is the basis of her work is of religious origin. Beda Alleman, in his essay *Allusion to a Poetic Realm,* demonstrated that she has taken the Cabala as her model, especially *The Sohar,* a commentary on the Pentateuch.

Then wrote the scribe of The Sohar
opening the words' mesh of veins
instilling blood from stars.

Thus begins a poem-sequence by Nelly Sachs which manifests the heritage that Alleman discusses. Book and inscription, archive and alphabet: these are concepts that recur throughout her work. They do not signify anything literary, but rather make literal use of the old concept of the book of nature, and, as it were, turn it around: the poetess does not copy nature's signs into her poems; she absorbs them so as to delineate future patterns:

The alphabet's corpse rose from the grave,
alphabet angel, ancient crystal,
immured by creation in drops of water
. . .
And unwraps, as though it were linen sheets
in which birth and death are swathed,
the alphabet womb, chrysalis
of green and red and white obscurity.

Nelly Sachs's *book* unfolds itself, gradually, with its language. Nothing in it is isolated; from one poem to the next the concrete detail is reiterated until its cosmic connotations are established. One of the varied images revealed throughout the book expresses this process itself: the image of the butterfly. The work itself is "alphabet's corpse" and "chrysalis." This summer creature appears first in the early poem *Chorus of the Unborn,* though still in the form of a seemingly conventional simile, as a metaphor pure and simple:

We are caught
Like butterflies by the sentries of your yearning—

In a later poem from *And No One Knows How to Go On* the image is elaborated:

All lands are ready to rise
from the map . . .
Ready to carry the last weight
of melancholy in a suitcase, this chrysalis
on the wings of which they will one day
end their journey.

What has, as it were, been enclosed in this image from the very beginning liberates itself finally and enters one of the central themes of Nelly Sachs's work, the theme of metamorphosis:

Fleeing,
what a great reception
on the way—
. . .
The sick butterfly
will soon learn again of the sea—
This stone
with the fly's inscription
gave itself into my hand—
I hold instead of a homeland
the metamorphoses of the world—

Not only the objects that appear in Nelly Sachs's book but even the words and images are subject to this law of transformation. For one of her most perfect poems, *Butterfly,* becomes both theme and title. This poem says:

What lovely aftermath
is painted in your dust.
What royal sign
in the secret of the air.

The image of the butterfly and the idea of creation as sign and inscription here combine with another basic word, which can be traced from the beginning to the end of her work: the word "dust." As an example of this, let us follow how one can read the word "dust" in this book, its course and its transformations from the first to the last poem.

At the beginning of this course stands not a metaphor but the black reality of our epoch. So the first poem of this book begins:

O the chimneys
On the ingeniously devised habitations of death
When Israel's body drifted as smoke
Through the air—
. . .
O the chimneys!
Freedomway for Jeremiah and Job's dust—

Dust, ashes, smoke stand with terrible exactness and concreteness above the crematory ovens of the German concentration camps. This is the beginning that is asserted throughout all transformations of dust, which is never forgotten and is always part of the thought. It is handed on expressly in the poem *To You That Build the New House:*

Oh, the walls and household utensils
Are responsive as Aeolian harps
Or like the field in which your sorrow grows,
And they sense your kinship with dust.

Build, when the hourglass trickles,
But do not weep away the minutes
Together with the dust
That obscures the light.

Dust is also the sand in the hourglass; it becomes the image of transitoriness as such. Not human kind alone, the whole earth is dust, and all creatures with it; dust in which life leaves its impression, its sign, its inscription as a trace, which can be read from the wings of the butterfly like this image:

But who emptied your shoes of sand
When you had to get up, to die?
The sand which Israel gathered,
Its nomad sand?
Burning Sinai sand,
Mingled with throats of nightingales,
Mingled with wings of butterflies . . .

As sand the dust is at home in the desert, where, in other words, no shelter exists whatsoever. The home in the homelessness of the desert is baptized Israel. Nelly Sachs is the last poetess of Jewry who writes in German, and her work remains incomprehensible without this royal origin. In her Stockholm refuge she experienced the genocide of the Final Solution more closely than we who lived near the death camps, and her book remains the only poetic testimony that can hold its own beside the dumfounding horror of the documentary reports. As incomparable as this poetic deed may be, one cannot confine her work within this achievement. It is to do an injustice to this work if one seeks to reduce it to this act of witnessing, to this lament, or even to supplying redeeming information for "overcoming" what no power can overcome.

To Nelly Sachs as to the ancient writings, Israel is representative of the story of all of creation's fortune and misfortune. Dust, smoke, ashes are not the "past," which one might be able to have done with, but are always contemporaneous. Today as well and every day it says:

The chimneys fly black flags
at the grave of air.
But man has said Ah
and climbs
a straight candle
into the night.

And even the stone partakes of the "metamorphoses of the world."

While the cricket scratches softly
at the invisible
and the stone dancing
changes its dust to music.

The path that this book traverses begins in flight and ends as a *Journey into a Dustless Realm:* this is the title of a later sequence of poems which the poetess also used for the edition of her collected poems. So palpable as the naked reality of the ashes and smoke in the extermination camps, so concretely begins the journey, as exile, dispossessed banishment, flight from the henchmen of 1940 into peaceful Sweden, and like the dust this journey ends as a cosmic one, as an image of the world.

Inscription, butterfly, metamorphosis, flight: as these elements of her poetry unfold themselves and intertwine, so do all the words that stand in this book. Wherever the reader begins, with the metaphor of hair and fire, the hunter and the hunted, sea and wings, or finger and shoe: from every point the "words' mesh of veins" will open up to him, and even the most daring telescoping of expression, the cryptically condensed stanza will become transparent to him when he traces the multifariousness of this coral reef of images. This poetry is also cabalistic in this linguistic sense: as the work of a magical *ars combinatora* that knows how to grasp even the incommensurable ever more lightly the more remote it is.

So this "royal word written far away" ought to become readable even if the book,

> *This chain of enigmas*
> *hung on the neck of night,*

will maintain its manifest secret against everyone who reads it, and thus will live on.

March 1963

Translators

The work of the various translators is identified in the table of contents as follows:

MH	Michael Hamburger
CH	Christopher Holme
RMM	Ruth and Matthew Mead
MR	Michael Roloff

As indicated, all of *Glowing Enigmas: I, II* and *III* was translated by Mr. Hamburger, and all of the verse play *Eli,* by Mr. Holme.

Contents

For purposes of simplification, only the page numbers of the English translations are given here. The German text will be found on the facing page.

Eclipse of the Stars

And No One Knows How to Go On

Journey into a Dustless Realm

Death Still Celebrates Life

Glowing Enigmas: II MH

In the Habitations of Death

For my dead brothers and sisters

O die Schornsteine

Und wenn diese meine Haut zerschlagen sein wird, so werde ich ohne mein Fleisch Gott schauen.—HIOB

O die Schornsteine
Auf den sinnreich erdachten Wohnungen des Todes,
Als Israels Leib zog aufgelöst in Rauch
Durch die Luft—
Als Essenkehrer ihn ein Stern empfing
Der schwarz wurde
Oder war es ein Sonnenstrahl?

O die Schornsteine!
Freiheitswege für Jeremias und Hiobs Staub—
Wer erdachte euch und baute Stein auf Stein
Den Weg für Flüchtlinge aus Rauch?

O die Wohnungen des Todes,
Einladend hergerichtet
Für den Wirt des Hauses, der sonst Gast war—
O ihr Finger,
Die Eingangsschwelle legend
Wie ein Messer zwischen Leben und Tod—

O ihr Schornsteine,
O ihr Finger,
Und Israels Leib im Rauch durch die Luft!

O the chimneys

And though after my skin worms destroy this body, yet in my flesh shall I see God.—JOB, 19:26

O the chimneys
On the ingeniously devised habitations of death
When Israel's body drifted as smoke
Through the air—
Was welcomed by a star, a chimney sweep,
A star that turned black
Or was it a ray of sun?

O the chimneys!
Freedomway for Jeremiah and Job's dust—
Who devised you and laid stone upon stone
The road for refugees of smoke?

O the habitations of death,
Invitingly appointed
For the host who used to be a guest—
O you fingers
Laying the threshold
Like a knife between life and death—

O you chimneys,
O you fingers
And Israel's body as smoke through the air!

An euch, die das neue Haus bauen

Es gibt Steine wie Seelen.—RABBI NACHMAN

Wenn du dir deine Wände neu aufrichtest—
Deinen Herd, Schlafstatt, Tisch und Stuhl—
Hänge nicht deine Tränen um sie, die dahingegangen,
Die nicht mehr mit dir wohnen werden
An den Stein
Nicht an das Holz—
Es weint sonst in deinen Schlaf hinein,
Den kurzen, den du noch tun musst.

Seufze nicht, wenn du dein Laken bettest,
Es mischen sich sonst deine Träume
Mit dem Schweiss der Toten.

Ach, es sind die Wände und die Geräte
Wie die Windharfen empfänglich
Und wie ein Acker, darin dein Leid wächst,
Und spüren das Staubverwandte in dir.

Baue, wenn die Stundenuhr rieselt,
Aber weine nicht die Minuten fort
Mit dem Staub zusammen,
Der das Licht verdeckt.

To you that build the new house

"There are stones like souls"—Rabbi Nachman

When you come to put up your walls anew—
Your stove, your bedstead, table and chair—
Do not hang your tears for those who departed,
Who will not live with you then,
On to the stone.
Nor on the timber—
Else weeping will pierce the sleep,
The brief sleep you have yet to take.

Do not sigh when you bed your sheets,
Else your dreams will mingle
With the sweat of the dead.

Oh, the walls and household utensils
Are responsive as Aeolian harps
Or like a field in which your sorrow grows,
And they sense your kinship with dust.

Build, when the hourglass trickles,
But do not weep away the minutes
Together with the dust
That obscures the light.

O der weinenden Kinder Nacht!

O der weinenden Kinder Nacht!
Der zum Tode gezeichneten Kinder Nacht!
Der Schlaf hat keinen Eingang mehr.
Schreckliche Wärterinnen
Sind an die Stelle der Mütter getreten,
Haben den falschen Tod in ihre Handmuskeln gespannt,
Säen ihn in die Wände und ins Gebälk—
Überall brütet es in den Nestern des Grauens.
Angst säugt die Kleinen statt der Muttermilch.

Zog die Mutter noch gestern
Wie ein weisser Mond den Schlaf heran,
Kam die Puppe mit dem fortgeküssten Wangenrot
In den einen Arm,
Kam das ausgestopfte Tier, lebendig
In der Liebe schon geworden,
In den andern Arm,—
Weht nun der Wind des Sterbens,
Bläst die Hemden über die Haare fort,
Die niemand mehr kämmen wird.

O the night of the weeping children!

O the night of the weeping children!
O the night of the children branded for death!
Sleep may not enter here.
Terrible nursemaids
Have usurped the place of mothers,
Have tautened their tendons with the false death,
Sow it on to the walls and into the beams—
Everywhere it is hatched in the nests of horror.
Instead of mother's milk, panic suckles those little ones.

Yesterday Mother still drew
Sleep toward them like a white moon,
There was the doll with cheeks derouged by kisses
In one arm,
The stuffed pet, already
Brought to life by love,
In the other—
Now blows the wind of dying,
Blows the shifts over the hair
That no one will comb again.

Wer aber leerte den Sand aus euren Schuhen

Wer aber leerte den Sand aus euren Schuhen,
Als ihr zum Sterben aufstehen musstet?
Den Sand, den Israel heimholte,
Seinen Wandersand?
Brennenden Sinaisand,
Mit den Kehlen von Nachtigallen vermischt,
Mit den Flügeln des Schmetterlings vermischt,
Mit dem Sehnsuchtsstaub der Schlangen vermischt,
Mit allem was abfiel von der Weisheit Salomos vermischt,
Mit dem Bitteren aus des Wermuts Geheimnis vermischt—

O ihr Finger,
Die ihr den Sand aus Totenschuhen leertet,
Morgen schon werdet ihr Staub sein
In den Schuhen Kommender!

But who emptied your shoes of sand

But who emptied your shoes of sand
When you had to get up, to die?
The sand which Israel gathered,
Its nomad sand?
Burning Sinai sand,
Mingled with throats of nightingales,
Mingled with wings of butterflies,
Mingled with the hungry dust of serpents;
Mingled with all that fell from the wisdom of Solomon,
Mingled with what is bitter in the mystery of wormwood—

O you fingers
That emptied the deathly shoes of sand.
Tomorrow you will be dust
In the shoes of those to come.

Auch der Greise

Auch der Greise
Letzten Atemzug, der schon den Tod anblies
Raubtet ihr noch fort.
Die leere Luft,
Zitternd vor Erwartung, den Seufzer der Erleichterung
Zu erfüllen, mit dem diese Erde fortgestossen wird—
Die leere Luft habt ihr beraubt!

Der Greise
Ausgetrocknetes Auge
Habt ihr noch einmal zusammengepresst
Bis ihr das Salz der Verzweiflung gewonnen hattet—
Alles was dieser Stern
An Krümmungen der Qual besitzt,
Alles Leiden aus den dunklen Verliesen der Würmer
Sammelte sich zuhauf—

O ihr Räuber von echten Todesstunden,
Letzten Atemzügen und der Augenlider *Gute Nacht*
Eines sei euch gewiss:

Es sammelt der Engel ein
Was ihr fortwarft,
Aus der Greise verfrühter Mitternacht
Wird sich ein Wind der letzten Atemzüge auftun,
Der diesen losgerissenen Stern
In seines Herrn Hände jagen wird!

Even the old men's last breath

Even the old men's last breath
That had already grazed death
You snatched away.
The empty air
Trembling
To fill the sigh of relief
That thrusts this earth away—
You have plundered the empty air!

The old men's
Parched eyes
You pressed once more
Till you reaped the salt of despair—
All that this star owns
Of the contortions of agony,
All suffering from the dungeons of worms
Gathered in heaps—

O you thieves of genuine hours of death,
Last breaths and the eyelids' Good Night
Of one thing be sure:

The angel, it gathers
What you discarded,
From the old men's premature midnight
A wind of last breaths shall arise
And drive this unloosed star
Into its Lord's hands!

Ein totes Kind spricht

Die Mutter hielt mich an der Hand.
Dann hob Jemand das Abschiedsmesser:
Die Mutter löste ihre Hand aus der meinen,
Damit es mich nicht träfe.
Sie aber berührte noch einmal leise meine Hüfte–
Und da blutete ihre Hand–

Von da ab schnitt mir das Abschiedsmesser
Den Bissen in der Kehle entzwei–
Es fuhr in der Morgendämmerung mit der Sonne hervor
Und begann, sich in meinen Augen zu schärfen–
In meinem Ohr schliffen sich Winde und Wasser,
Und jede Trostesstimme stach in mein Herz–

Als man mich zum Tode führte,
Fühlte ich im letzten Augenblick noch
Das Herausziehen des grossen Abschiedsmessers.

A dead child speaks

My mother held me by my hand.
Then someone raised the knife of parting:
So that it should not strike me,
My mother loosed her hand from mine.
But she lightly touched my thighs once more
And her hand was bleeding–

After that the knife of parting
Cut in two each bite I swallowed–
It rose before me with the sun at dawn
And began to sharpen itself in my eyes–
Wind and water ground in my ear
And every voice of comfort pierced my heart–

As I was led to death
I still felt in the last moment
The unsheathing of the great knife of parting.

Schon vom Arm des himmlischen Trostes umfangen

Schon vom Arm des himmlischen Trostes umfangen
Steht die wahnsinnige Mutter
Mit den Fetzen ihres zerrissenen Verstandes,
Mit den Zundern ihres verbrannten Verstandes
Ihr totes Kind einsargend,
Ihr verlorenes Licht einsargend,
Ihre Hände zu Krügen biegend,
Aus der Luft füllend mit dem Leib ihres Kindes,
Aus der Luft füllend mit seinen Augen, seinen Haaren
Und seinem flatternden Herzen—

Dann küsst sie das Luftgeborene
Und stirbt!

Already embraced by the arm of heavenly solace

Already embraced by the arm of heavenly solace
The insane mother stands
With the tatters of her torn mind
With the charred tinders of her burnt mind
Burying her dead child,
Burying her lost light,
Twisting her hands into urns,
Filling them with the body of her child from the air,
Filling them with his eyes, his hair from the air,
And with his fluttering heart—

Then she kisses the air-born being
And dies!

Welche geheimen Wünsche des Blutes

Welche geheimen Wünsche des Blutes,
Träume des Wahnes und tausendfach
Gemordetes Erdreich
Liessen den schrecklichen Marionettenspieler entstehen?

Er, der mit schäumendem Munde
Furchtbar umblies
Die runde, kreisende Bühne seiner Tat
Mit dem aschgrau ziehenden Horizont der Angst!

O die Staubhügel, die, wie von bösem Mond gezogen
Die Mörder spielten:

Arme auf und ab,
Beine auf und ab
Und die untergehende Sonne des Sinaivolkes
Als den roten Teppich unter den Füssen.

Arme auf und ab,
Beine auf und ab
Und am ziehenden aschgrauen Horizont der Angst
Riesengross das Gestirn des Todes
Wie die Uhr der Zeiten stehend.

What secret cravings of the blood

What secret cravings of the blood,
Dreams of madness and earth
A thousand times murdered,
Brought into being the terrible puppeteer?

Him who with foaming mouth
Dreadfully swept away
The round, the circling stage of his deed
With the ash-gray, receding horizon of fear?

O the hills of dust, which as though drawn by an evil moon
The murderers enacted:

Arms up and down,
Legs up and down
And the setting sun of Sinai's people
A red carpet under their feet.

Arms up and down,
Legs up and down
And on the ash-gray receding horizon of fear
Gigantic the constellation of death
That loomed like the clock face of ages.

Ihr Zuschauenden

Unter deren Blicken getötet wurde.
Wie man auch einen Blick im Rücken fühlt,
So fühlt ihr an euerm Leibe
Die Blicke der Toten.

Wieviel brechende Augen werden euch ansehn
Wenn ihr aus den Verstecken ein Veilchen pflückt?
Wieviel flehend erhobene Hände
In dem märtyrerhaft geschlungenen Gezweige
Der alten Eichen?
Wieviel Erinnerung wächst im Blute
Der Abendsonne?

O die ungesungenen Wiegenlieder
In der Turteltaube Nachtruf—
Manch einer hätte Sterne herunterholen können,
Nun muss es der alte Brunnen für ihn tun!

Ihr Zuschauenden,
Die ihr keine Mörderhand erhobt,
Aber die ihr den Staub nicht von eurer Sehnsucht
Schütteltet,
Die ihr stehenbliebt, dort, wo er zu Licht
Verwandelt wird.

You onlookers

Whose eyes watched the killing.
As one feels a stare at one's back
You feel on your bodies
The glances of the dead.

How many dying eyes will look at you
When you pluck a violet from its hiding place?
How many hands be raised in supplication
In the twisted martyr-like branches
Of old oaks?
How much memory grows in the blood
Of the evening sun?

O the unsung cradlesongs
In the night cry of the turtledove–
Many a one might have plucked stars from the sky,
Now the old well must do it for them!

You onlookers,
You who raised no hand in murder,
But who did not shake the dust
From your longing,
You who halted there, where dust is changed
To light.

Qual, Zeitmesser eines fremden Sterns

Die Gewänder des Morgens sind nicht
die Gewänder des Abends.—Buch Sohar

Qual, Zeitmesser eines fremden Sterns,
Jede Minute mit anderem Dunkel färbend—
Qual deiner erbrochenen Tür,
Deines erbrochenen Schlafes,
Deiner fortgehenden Schritte,
Die das letzte Leben hinzählten,
Deiner zertretenen Schritte,
Deiner schleifenden Schritte,
Bis sie aufhörten Schritte zu sein für mein Ohr.
Qual um das Ende deiner Schritte
Vor einem Gitter,
Dahinter die Flur unserer Sehnsucht zu wogen begann—
O Zeit, die nur nach Sterben rechnet,
Wie leicht wird Tod nach dieser langen Übung sein.

Agony, metronome of an alien star

The robes of morning are not the robes of evening.—The Sohar

Agony, metronome of an alien star,
Staining each minute with a different darkness—
Agony of your broken door,
Your broken sleep,
Your departing steps
That counted out the remains of life,
Of your crushed steps,
Your dragging steps,
Till they ceased being steps to my ear.
Agony of the end of your steps
Before an iron grate
Behind which the meadow of our yearning began to sway—
O time whose only measurement is dying,
How easy death will be after this long rehearsal.

Wenn ich nur wüsste

Wenn ich nur wüsste,
Worauf dein letzter Blick ruhte.
War es ein Stein, der schon viele letzte Blicke
Getrunken hatte, bis sie in Blindheit
Auf den Blinden fielen?

Oder war es Erde,
Genug, um einen Schuh zu füllen,
Und schon schwarz geworden
Von soviel Abschied
Und von soviel Tod bereiten?

Oder war es dein letzter Weg,
Der dir das Lebewohl von allen Wegen brachte
Die du gegangen warst?

Eine Wasserlache, ein Stück spiegelndes Metall,
Vielleicht die Gürtelschnalle deines Feindes,
Oder irgend ein anderer, kleiner Wahrsager
Des Himmels?

Oder sandte dir diese Erde,
Die keinen ungeliebt von hinnen gehen lässt
Ein Vogelzeichen durch die Luft,
Erinnernd deine Seele, dass sie zuckte
In ihrem qualverbrannten Leib?

If I only knew

If I only knew
On what your last look rested.
Was it a stone that had drunk
So many last looks that they fell
Blindly upon its blindness?

Or was it earth,
Enough to fill a shoe,
And black already
With so much parting
And with so much killing?

Or was it your last road
That brought you a farewell from all the roads
You had walked?

A puddle, a bit of shining metal,
Perhaps the buckle of your enemy's belt,
Or some other small augury
Of heaven?

Or did this earth,
Which lets no one depart unloved,
Send you a bird-sign through the air,
Reminding your soul that it quivered
In the torment of its burnt body?

Chor der Geretteten

Wir Geretteten,
Aus deren hohlem Gebein der Tod schon seine Flöten schnitt,
An deren Sehnen der Tod schon seinen Bogen strich—
Unsere Leiber klagen noch nach
Mit ihrer verstümmelten Musik.
Wir Geretteten,
Immer noch hängen die Schlingen für unsere Hälse gedreht
Vor uns in der blauen Luft—
Immer noch füllen sich die Stundenuhren mit unserem
tropfenden Blut.
Wir Geretteten,
Immer noch essen an uns die Würmer der Angst.
Unser Gestirn ist vergraben im Staub.
Wir Geretteten
Bitten euch:
Zeigt uns langsam eure Sonne.
Führt uns von Stern zu Stern im Schritt.
Lasst uns das Leben leise wieder lernen.
Es könnte sonst eines Vogels Lied,
Das Füllen des Eimers am Brunnen
Unseren schlecht versiegelten Schmerz aufbrechen lassen
Und uns wegschäumen—
Wir bitten euch:
Zeigt uns noch nicht einen beissenden Hund—
Es könnte sein, es könnte sein
Dass wir zu Staub zerfallen—
Vor euren Augen zerfallen in Staub.
Was hält denn unsere Webe zusammen?

Chorus of the Rescued

We, the rescued,
From whose hollow bones death had begun to whittle his
flutes,
And on whose sinews he had already stroked his bow—
Our bodies continue to lament
With their mutilated music.
We, the rescued,
The nooses wound for our necks still dangle
before us in the blue air—
Hourglasses still fill with our dripping blood.
We, the rescued,
The worms of fear still feed on us.
Our constellation is buried in dust.
We, the rescued,
Beg you:
Show us your sun, but gradually.
Lead us from star to star, step by step.
Be gentle when you teach us to live again.
Lest the song of a bird,
Or a pail being filled at the well,
Let our badly sealed pain burst forth again
and carry us away—
We beg you:
Do not show us an angry dog, not yet—
It could be, it could be
That we will dissolve into dust—
Dissolve into dust before your eyes.
For what binds our fabric together?

Wir odemlos gewordene,
Deren Seele zu Ihm floh aus der Mitternacht
Lange bevor man unseren Leib rettete
In die Arche des Augenblicks.
Wir Geretteten,
Wir drücken eure Hand,
Wir erkennen euer Auge—
Aber zusammen hält uns nur noch der Abschied,
Der Abschied im Staub
Hält uns mit euch zusammen.

We whose breath vacated us,
Whose soul fled to Him out of that midnight
Long before our bodies were rescued
Into the ark of the moment.
We, the rescued,
We press your hand
We look into your eye—
But all that binds us together now is leave-taking,
The leave-taking in the dust
Binds us together with you.

Chor der Waisen

Wir Waisen
Wir klagen der Welt:
Herabgehauen hat man unseren Ast
Und ins Feuer geworfen–
Brennholz hat man aus unseren Beschützern gemacht–
Wir Waisen liegen auf den Feldern der Einsamkeit.
Wir Waisen
Wir klagen der Welt:
In der Nacht spielen unsere Eltern Verstecken mit uns–
Hinter den schwarzen Falten der Nacht
Schauen uns ihre Gesichter an,
Sprechen ihre Münder:
Dürrholz waren wir in eines Holzhauers Hand–
Aber unsere Augen sind Engelaugen geworden
Und sehen euch an,
Durch die schwarzen Falten der Nacht
Blicken sie hindurch–
Wir Waisen
Wir klagen der Welt:
Steine sind unser Spielzeug geworden,
Steine haben Gesichter, Vater- und Muttergesichter
Sie verwelken nicht wie Blumen, sie beissen nicht wie Tiere–
Und sie brennen nicht wie Dürrholz, wenn man sie in den
        Ofen wirft–
Wir Waisen wir klagen der Welt:

Chorus of the Orphans

We orphans
We lament to the world:
Our branch has been cut down
And thrown in the fire—
Kindling was made of our protectors—
We orphans lie stretched out on the fields of loneliness.
We orphans
We lament to the world:
At night our parents play hide and seek—
From behind the black folds of night
Their faces gaze at us,
Their mouths speak:
Kindling we were in a woodcutter's hand—
But our eyes have become angel eyes
And regard you,
Through the black folds of night
They penetrate—
We orphans
We lament to the world:
Stones have become our playthings,
Stones have faces, father and mother faces
They wilt not like flowers, nor bite like beasts—
And burn not like tinder when tossed into the oven—
We orphans we lament to the world:

Welt warum hast du uns die weichen Mütter genommen
Und die Väter, die sagen: Mein Kind du gleichst mir!
Wir Waisen gleichen niemand mehr auf der Welt!
O Welt
Wir klagen dich an!

World, why have you taken our soft mothers from us
And the fathers who say: My child, you are like me!
We orphans are like no one in this world any more!
O world
We accuse you!

Chor der Schatten

Wir Schatten, o wir Schatten!
Schatten von Henkern
Geheftet am Staube eurer Untaten—
Schatten von Opfern
Zeichnend das Drama eures Blutes an eine Wand.
O wir hilflosen Trauerfalter
Eingefangen auf einem Stern, der ruhig weiterbrennt
Wenn wir in Höllen tanzen müssen.
Unsere Marionettenspieler wissen nur noch den Tod.

Goldene Amme, die du uns nährst
Zu solcher Verzweiflung,
Wende ab o Sonne dein Angesicht
Auf dass auch wir versinken—
Oder lass uns spiegeln eines Kindes jauchzend
Erhobene Finger
Und einer Libelle leichtes Glück
Über dem Brunnenrand.

Chorus of the Shadows

We shadows, O we shadows!
Shadows of hangmen
Pinned to the dust of your crimes—
Shadows of victims
Silhouetting the drama of your blood on a wall.
O we helpless moths of mourning
Caught in a star that calmly goes on burning
When we must dance in hell.
Our puppeteers know nothing but death any more.

Golden nurse, you who feed us
For such despair,
Turn away, O sun, your countenance
So that we too may sink away—
Or let us mirror a child's
Fingers raised in joy
And a dragonfly's flimsy luck
Above the rim of a well.

Chor der Steine

Wir Steine
Wenn einer uns hebt
Hebt er Urzeiten empor–
Wenn einer uns hebt
Hebt er den Garten Eden empor–
Wenn einer uns hebt
Hebt er Adam und Evas Erkenntnis empor
Und der Schlange staubessende Verführung.

Wenn einer uns hebt
Hebt er Billionen Erinnerungen in seiner Hand
Die sich nicht auflösen im Blute
Wie der Abend.
Denn Gedenksteine sind wir
Alles Sterben umfassend.

Ein Ranzen voll gelebten Lebens sind wir.
Wer uns hebt, hebt die hartgewordenen Gräber der Erde.
Ihr Jakobshäupter,
Die Wurzeln der Träume halten wir versteckt für euch,
Lassen die luftigen Engelsleitern
Wie Ranken eines Windenbeetes spriessen.

Chorus of the Stones

We stones
When someone lifts us
He lifts the Foretime—
When someone lifts us
He lifts the Garden of Eden—
When someone lifts us
He lifts the knowledge of Adam and Eve
And the serpent's dust-eating seduction.

When someone lifts us
He lifts in his hand millions of memories
Which do not dissolve in blood
Like evening.
For we are memorial stones
Embracing all dying.

We are a satchel full of lived life.
Whoever lifts us lifts the hardened graves of earth.
You heads of Jacob,
For you we hide the roots of dreams
And let the airy angels' ladders
Sprout like the tendrils of a bed of bindweed.

Wenn einer uns anrührt
Rührt er eine Klagemauer an.
Wie der Diamant zerschneidet eure Klage unsere Härte
Bis sie zerfällt und weiches Herz wird—
Während ihr versteint.
Wenn einer uns anrührt
Rührt er die Wegscheiden der Mitternacht an
Klingend von Geburt und Tod.

Wenn einer uns wirft—
Wirft er den Garten Eden—
Den Wein der Sterne—
Die Augen der Liebenden und allen Verrat—

Wenn einer uns wirft im Zorne
So wirft er Äonen gebrochener Herzen
Und seidener Schmetterlinge.

Hütet euch, hütet euch
Zu werfen im Zorne mit einem Stein—
Unser Gemisch ist ein vom Odem Durchblasenes.
Es erstarrte im Geheimnis
Aber kann erwachen an einem Kuss.

When someone touches us
He touches the wailing wall.
Like a diamond your lament cuts our hardness
Until it crumbles and becomes a soft heart—
While you turn to stone.
When someone touches us
He touches the forked ways of midnight
Sounding with birth and death.

When someone throws us—
He throws the Garden of Eden—
The wine of the stars—
The eyes of the lovers and all betrayal—

When someone throws us in anger
He throws aeons of broken hearts
And silken butterflies.

Beware, beware
Of throwing a stone in anger—
Breath once transfused our minglement,
Which grew solid in secret
But can awaken at a kiss.

Chor der Sterne

Wir Sterne, wir Sterne
Wir wandernder, glänzender, singender Staub—
Unsere Schwester die Erde ist die Blinde geworden
Unter den Leuchtbildern des Himmels—
Ein Schrei ist sie geworden
Unter den Singenden—
Sie, die Sehnsuchtsvollste
Die im Staube begann ihr Werk: Engel zu bilden—
Sie, die die Seligkeit in ihrem Geheimnis trägt
Wie goldführendes Gewässer—
Ausgeschüttet in der Nacht liegt sie
Wie Wein auf den Gassen—
Des Bösen gelbe Schwefellichter hüpfen auf ihrem Leib.

O Erde, Erde
Stern aller Sterne
Durchzogen von den Spuren des Heimwehs
Die Gott selbst begann—
Ist niemand auf dir, der sich erinnert an deine Jugend?
Niemand, der sich hingibt als Schwimmer
Den Meeren von Tod?
Ist niemandes Sehnsucht reif geworden
Dass sie sich erhebt wie der engelhaft fliegende Samen
Der Löwenzahnblüte?

Erde, Erde, bist du eine Blinde geworden
Vor den Schwesternaugen der Plejaden
Oder der Waage prüfendem Blick?

Chorus of the Stars

We stars, we stars
We wandering, glistening, singing dust—
Earth, our sister, has gone blind
Among the constellations of heaven—
A scream she has become
Among the singers—
She, richest in longing
Who began her task—to form angels—in dust,
She whose secret contains bliss
Like streams bearing gold—
Poured out into the night she lies
Like wine in the streets—
Evil's yellow sulfur lights flicker over her body.

O earth, earth
Star of stars
Veined by the spoors of homesickness
Begun by God Himself—
Have you no one who remembers your youth?
No one who will surrender himself as the swimmer
To the oceans of death?
Has no one's longing ripened
So it will rise like the angelically flying seed
Of the dandelion blossom?

Earth, earth, have you gone blind
Before the sister eyes of the Pleiades
Or Libra's examining gaze?

Mörderhände gaben Israel einen Spiegel
Darin es sterbend sein Sterben erblickte—

Erde, o Erde
Stern aller Sterne
Einmal wird ein Sternbild Spiegel heissen.
Dann o Blinde wirst du wieder sehn!

Murder hands gave Israel a mirror
In which it recognized its death while dying—

Earth, O earth
Star of stars
One day a constellation will be called *mirror.*
Then, O blind one, you will see again!

Chor der Ungeborenen

Wir Ungeborenen
Schon beginnt die Sehnsucht an uns zu schaffen
Die Ufer des Blutes weiten sich zu unserem Empfang
Wie Tau sinken wir in die Liebe hinein.
Noch liegen die Schatten der Zeit wie Fragen
Über unserem Geheimnis.

Ihr Liebenden,
Ihr Sehnsüchtigen,
Hört, ihr Abschiedskranken:
Wir sind es, die in euren Blicken zu leben beginnen,
In euren Händen, die suchende sind in der blauen Luft—
Wir sind es, die nach Morgen Duftenden.
Schon zieht uns euer Atem ein,
Nimmt uns hinab in euren Schlaf
In die Träume, die unser Erdreich sind
Wo unsere schwarze Amme, die Nacht
Uns wachsen lässt,
Bis wir uns spiegeln in euren Augen
Bis wir sprechen in euer Ohr.

Schmetterlingsgleich
Werden wir von den Häschern eurer Sehnsucht gefangen—
Wie Vogelstimmen an die Erde verkauft—
Wir Morgenduftenden,
Wir kommenden Lichter für eure Traurigkeit.

Chorus of the Unborn

We the unborn
The yearning has begun to plague us
The shores of blood broaden to receive us
Like dew we sink into love
But still the shadows of time lie like questions
Over our secret.

You who love,
You who yearn,
Listen, you who are sick with parting:
We are those who begin to live in your glances,
In your hands which are searching the blue air—
We are those who smell of morning.
Already your breath is inhaling us,
Drawing us down into your sleep
Into the dreams which are our earth
Where night, our black nurse,
Lets us grow
Until we mirror ourselves in your eyes
Until we speak into your ear.

We are caught
Like butterflies by the sentries of your yearning—
Like birdsong sold to earth—
We who smell of morning,
We future lights for your sorrow.

Stimme des Heiligen Landes

O meine Kinder,
Der Tod ist durch eure Herzen gefahren
Wie durch einen Weinberg—
Malte *Israel* rot an alle Wände der Erde.

Wo soll die kleine Heiligkeit hin
Die noch in meinem Sande wohnt?
Durch die Röhren der Abgeschiedenheit
Sprechen die Stimmen der Toten:

Leget auf den Acker die Waffen der Rache
Damit sie leise werden—
Denn auch Eisen und Korn sind Geschwister
Im Schosse der Erde—

Wo soll denn die kleine Heiligkeit hin
Die noch in meinem Sande wohnt?

Das Kind im Schlafe gemordet
Steht auf; biegt den Baum der Jahrtausende hinab
Und heftet den weissen, atmenden Stern
Der einmal Israel hiess
An seine Krone.
Schnelle zurück, spricht es
Dorthin, wo Tränen Ewigkeit bedeuten.

The voice of the Holy Land

O my children,
Death has run through your hearts
As through a vineyard—
Painted *Israel* red on all the walls of the world.

What shall be the end of the little holiness
Which still dwells in my sand?
The voices of the dead
Speak through reed pipes of seclusion.

Lay the weapons of revenge in the field
That they grow gentle—
For even iron and grain are akin
In the womb of earth—

But what shall be the end of the little holiness
Which still dwells in my sand?

The child murdered in sleep
Arises; bends down the tree of ages
And pins the white breathing star
That was once called Israel
To its topmost bough.
Spring upright again, says the child,
To where tears mean eternity.

Eclipse of the Stars

In memory of my father

Wenn wie Rauch der Schlaf einzieht in den Leib

Wenn wie Rauch der Schlaf einzieht in den Leib,
und wie ein erloschenes Gestirn, das anderswo entzündet
wird,
der Mensch zu Grunde fährt,
steht der Streit still,
abgetriebene Mähre, die den Albdruck ihres Reiters
abgeworfen hat.
Aus ihrem heimlichen Takt entlassen
sind die Schritte,
die wie Brunnenschwengel an das Rätsel der Erde klopften.
Alle künstlichen Tode sind in ihre blutverwirrten Nester
heimgekehrt.

Wenn wie Rauch der Schlaf einzieht in den Leib,
atmet das Kind gestillt, mit der Mondtrompete im Arm.
Die Träne verschläft ihre Sehnsucht zu fliessen,
aber die Liebe ist alle Umwege zu Ende gegangen
und ruht in ihrem Beginn.
Jetzt ist die Zeit für das Kalb seine neue Zunge
am Leib der Mutter zu proben,
der falsche Schlüssel schliesst nicht
und das Messer rostet hinein
bis in die blasse Heide der Morgendämmerung
die aus der Vergessenheit erblüht im furchtbaren Frühröt.

When sleep enters the body like smoke

When sleep enters the body like smoke
and man journeys into the abyss
like an extinguished star that is lighted elsewhere,
then all quarrel ceases,
overworked nag that has tossed the nightmare grip
of its rider.
Released from their secret rhythm
are the steps
that knock like well lifts at the earth's enigma.
All artificial deaths have returned to the bloody confusion
of their nests.

When sleep enters the body like smoke
the stilled child breathes with the moon trumpet in its arm.
The tear oversleeps its longing to flow,
but love has completed all detours
and rests in its beginning.
Now is the time for the calf to test
its new tongue on its mother's body,
the wrong key does not lock
and the knife rusts far
into the pale heath of dawn
which blossoms out of the oblivion
with the early morning's fearful red.

Wenn wie Rauch der Schlaf auszieht aus dem Leib,
und der Mensch geheimnisgesättigt
die abgetriebene Mähre des Streites
aus dem Stalle treibt,
beginnt die feuerschnaubende Verbindung aufs neue
und der Tod erwacht in jeder Maienknospe
und das Kind küsst einen Stein
in der Sternverdunkelung.

When sleep leaves the body like smoke
and man, sated with secrets,
drives the overworked nag of quarrel
out of its stall,
then the fire-breathing union begins anew
and death wakens in every bud of May
and the child kisses a stone
in the eclipse of the stars.

Nacht, Nacht

Nacht, Nacht,
dass du nicht in Scherben zerspringst,
nun wo die Zeit mit den reissenden Sonnen
des Martyriums
in deiner meergedeckten Tiefe untergeht–
die Monde des Todes
das stürzende Erdendach
in deines Schweigens geronnenes Blut ziehn–

Nacht, Nacht,
einmal warst du der Geheimnisse Braut
schattenliliengeschmückt–
In deinem dunklen Glase glitzerte
die Fata Morgana der Sehnsüchtigen
und die Liebe hatte ihre Morgenrose
dir zum Erblühen hingestellt–
Einmal warst du der Traummalereien
jenseitiger Spiegel und orakelnder Mund–

Nacht, Nacht,
jetzt bist du der Friedhof
für eines Sternes schrecklichen Schiffbruch geworden–
sprachlos taucht die Zeit in dir unter
mit ihrem Zeichen:
Der stürzende Stein
und die Fahne aus Rauch!

Night, night

Night, night,
that you may not shatter in fragments
now when time sinks with the ravenous suns
of martyrdom
in your sea-covered depths—
the moons of death
drag the falling roof of earth
into the congealed blood of your silence.

Night, night,
once you were the bride of mysteries
adorned with lilies of shadow—
In your dark glass sparkled
the mirage of all who yearn
and love had set its morning rose
to blossom before you—
You were once the oracular mouth
of dream painting and mirrored the beyond.

Night, night,
now you are the graveyard
for the terrible shipwreck of a star—
time sinks speechless in you
with its sign:
The falling stone
and the flag of smoke.

Auf dass die Verfolgten nicht Verfolger werden

Schritte—
In welchen Grotten der Echos
seid ihr bewahrt,
die ihr den Ohren einst weissagtet
kommenden Tod?

Schritte—
Nicht Vogelflug, noch Schau der Eingeweide,
noch der blutschwitzende Mars
gab des Orakels Todesauskunft mehr—
nur Schritte—

Schritte—
Urzeitspiel von Henker und Opfer,
Verfolger und Verfolgten,
Jäger und Gejagt—

Schritte
die die Zeit reissend machen
die Stunde mit Wölfen behängen,
dem Flüchtling die Flucht auslöschen
im Blute.

Schritte
die Zeit zählend mit Schreien, Seufzern,
Austritt des Blutes bis es gerinnt,
Todesschweiss zu Stunden häufend—

That the persecuted may not become persecutors

Footsteps—
In which of Echo's grottoes
are you preserved,
you who once prophesied aloud
the coming of death?

Footsteps—
Neither bird-flight, inspection of entrails,
nor Mars sweating blood
confirmed the oracle's message of death—
only footsteps—

Footsteps—
Age-old game of hangman and victim,
Persecutor and persecuted,
Hunter and hunted—

Footsteps
which turn time ravenous
emblazoning the hour with wolves
extinguishing the flight in the fugitive's
blood.

Footsteps
measuring time with screams, groans,
the seeping of blood until it congeals,
heaping up hours of sweaty death—

Schritte der Henker
über Schritten der Opfer,
Sekundenzeiger im Gang der Erde,
von welchem Schwarzmond schrecklich gezogen?

In der Musik der Sphären
wo schrillt euer Ton?

Steps of hangmen
over the steps of victims,
what black moon pulled with such terror
the sweep-hand in earth's orbit?

Where does your note shrill
in the music of the spheres?

Wenn die Propheten einbrächen

Wenn die Propheten einbrächen
durch Türen der Nacht,
den Tierkreis der Dämonengötter
wie einen schauerlichen Blumenkranz
ums Haupt gewunden—
die Geheimnisse der stürzenden und sich hebenden
Himmel mit den Schultern wiegend—

für die längst vom Schauer Fortgezogenen—

Wenn die Propheten einbrächen
durch Türen der Nacht,
die Sternenstrassen gezogen in ihren Handflächen
golden aufleuchten lassend—

für die längst im Schlaf Versunkenen—

Wenn die Propheten einbrächen
durch Türen der Nacht
mit ihren Worten Wunden reissend
in die Felder der Gewohnheit,
ein weit Entlegenes hereinholend
für den Tagelöhner

der längst nicht mehr wartet am Abend—

If the prophets broke in

If the prophets broke in
through the doors of night,
the zodiac of demon gods
wound like a ghastly wreath of flowers
round the head—
rocking the secrets of the falling and rising
skies on their shoulders—

for those who long since fled in terror—

If the prophets broke in
through the doors of night,
the course of the stars scored in their palms
glowing golden—

for those long sunk in sleep—

If the prophets broke in
through the doors of night
tearing wounds with their words
into fields of habit,
a distant crop hauled home
for the laborer

who no longer waits at evening—

Wenn die Propheten einbrächen
durch Türen der Nacht
und ein Ohr wie eine Heimat suchten—

Ohr der Menschheit
du nesselverwachsenes,
würdest du hören?
Wenn die Stimme der Propheten
auf dem Flötengebein der ermordeten Kinder
blasen würde,
die vom Märtyrerschrei verbrannten Lüfte
ausatmete—
wenn sie eine Brücke aus verendeten Greisenseufzern
baute—

Ohr der Menschheit
du mit dem kleinen Lauschen beschäftigtes,
würdest du hören?

Wenn die Propheten
mit den Sturmschwingen der Ewigkeit hineinführen
wenn sie aufbrächen deinen Gehörgang mit den Worten:
Wer von euch will Krieg führen gegen ein Geheimnis
wer will den Sterntod erfinden?

Wenn die Propheten aufständen
in der Nacht der Menschheit
wie Liebende, die das Herz des Geliebten suchen,
Nacht der Menschheit
würdest du ein Herz zu vergeben haben?

If the prophets broke in
through the doors of night
and sought an ear like a homeland—

Ear of mankind
overgrown with nettles,
would you hear?
If the voice of the prophets
blew
on flutes made of murdered children's bones
and exhaled airs burnt with
martyrs' cries—
if they built a bridge of old men's dying
groans—

Ear of mankind
occupied with small sounds,
would you hear?

If the prophets
rushed in with the storm-pinions of eternity
if they broke open your acoustic duct with the words:
Which of you wants to make war against a mystery
who wants to invent the star-death?

If the prophets stood up
in the night of mankind
like lovers who seek the heart of the beloved,
night of mankind
would you have a heart to offer?

Hiob

O du Windrose der Qualen!
Von Urzeitstürmen
in immer andere Richtungen der Unwetter gerissen;
noch dein Süden heisst Einsamkeit.
Wo du stehst, ist der Nabel der Schmerzen.

Deine Augen sind tief in deinen Schädel gesunken
wie Höhlentauben in der Nacht
die der Jäger blind herausholt.
Deine Stimme ist stumm geworden,
denn sie hat zuviel *Warum* gefragt.

Zu den Würmern und Fischen ist deine Stimme eingegangen.
Hiob, du hast alle Nachtwachen durchweint
aber einmal wird das Sternbild deines Blutes
alle aufgehenden Sonnen erbleichen lassen.

Job

O you windrose of agonies!
Swept by primordial storms
always into other directions of inclemency;
even your South is called loneliness.
Where you stand is the navel of pain.

Your eyes have sunk deep into your skull
like cave doves which the hunter
fetches blindly at night.
Your voice has gone dumb,
having too often asked *why*.

Your voice has joined the worms and fishes.
Job, you have cried through all vigils
but one day the constellation of your blood
shall make all rising suns blanch.

Warum die schwarze Antwort des Hasses

Warum die schwarze Antwort des Hasses
auf dein Dasein, Israel?

Fremdling du,
einen Stern von weiterher
als die anderen.
Verkauft an diese Erde
damit Einsamkeit fort sich erbe.

Deine Herkunft verwachsen mit Unkraut—
deine Sterne vertauscht
gegen alles was Motten und Würmern gehört,
und doch von den Traumsandufern der Zeit
wie Mondwasser fortgeholt in die Ferne.

Im Chore der anderen
hast du gesungen
einen Ton höher
oder einen Ton tiefer—

der Abendsonne hast du dich ins Blut geworfen
wie ein Schmerz den anderen sucht.
Lang ist dein Schatten
und es ist späte Zeit für dich geworden
Israel!

Why the black answer of hate

Why the black answer of hate
to your existence, Israel?

You stranger
from a star one farther away
than the others.
Sold to this earth
that loneliness might be passed on.

Your origin entangled in weeds—
your stars bartered
for all that belongs to moths and worms,
and yet: fetched away from dreamfilled sandy shores of time
like moonwater into the distance.

In the others' choir
you always sang
one note lower
or one note higher—

you flung yourself into the blood of the evening sun
like one pain seeking the other.
Long is your shadow
and it has become late for you
Israel!

Wie weit dein Weg von der Segnung
den Äon der Tränen entlang
bis zu der Wegbiegung
da du in Asche gefallen,

dein Feind mit dem Rauch
deines verbrannten Leibes
deine Todverlassenheit
an die Stirn des Himmels schrieb!

O solcher Tod!
Wo alle helfenden Engel
mit blutenden Schwingen
zerrissen im Stacheldraht
der Zeit hingen!

Warum die schwarze Antwort des Hasses
auf dein Dasein
Israel?

How far your way from the blessing
along the aeon of tears
to the bend of the road
where you turned to ashes

and your enemy with the smoke
of your burned body
engraved your mortal abandonment
on the brow of heaven!

O such a death!
When all helping angels
with bleeding wings
hung tattered
in the barbed wire of time!

Why the black answer of hate
to your existence
Israel?

Israel

Israel,
namenloser einst,
noch von des Todes Efeu umsponnen,
arbeitete geheim die Ewigkeit in dir, traumtief
bestiegst du
der Mondtürme magische Spirale,
die mit Tiermasken verhüllten Gestirne
umkreisend–
in der Fische Mirakelstummheit
oder mit des Widders anstürmender Härte.

Bis der versiegelte Himmel aufbrach
und du,
Waghalsigster unter den Nachtwandlern,
getroffen von der Gotteswunde
in den Abgrund aus Licht fielst–

Israel,
Zenit der Sehnsucht,
gehäuft über deinem Haupte
ist das Wunder wie Gewitter,
entlädt sich im Schmerzgebirge deiner Zeit.

Israel,
erst zart, wie das Lied der Vögel
und leidender Kinder Gespräche
rinnt des lebendigen Gottes Quelle
heimatlich aus deinem Blut–

Israel

Israel,
more nameless then,
still ensnared in the ivy of death,
in you eternity worked secretly, dream-deep
you mounted
the enchanted spiral of the moon towers,
circling the constellations disguised
by animal masks—
in the mute miraculous silence of Pisces
or the battering charges of Aries.

Until the sealed sky broke open
and you,
most daredevil of sleepwalkers,
fell, struck by the wound of God
into the abyss of light—

Israel,
zenith of longing,
wonder is heaped
like a storm upon your head,
breaks in your time's mountains of pain.

Israel,
tender at first, like the song of a bird
and the talk of suffering children
the source of the living God,
a native spring,
flows from your blood.

Zahlen

Als eure Formen zu Asche versanken
in die Nachtmeere,
wo Ewigkeit in die Gezeiten
Leben und Tod spült—

erhoben sich Zahlen—
(gebrannt einmal in eure Arme
damit niemand der Qual entginge)

erhoben sich Meteore aus Zahlen,
gerufen in die Räume
darin Lichterjahre wie Pfeile sich strecken
und die Planeten
aus den magischen Stoffen
des Schmerzes geboren werden—

Zahlen—mit ihren Wurzeln
aus Mördergehirnen gezogen
und schon eingerechnet
in des himmlischen Kreislaufs
blaugeäderter Bahn.

Numbers

When your forms turned to ashes
into the oceans of night
where eternity washes
life and death into the tides—

there rose the numbers—
(once branded into your arms
so none would escape the agony)

there rose meteors of numbers
beckoned into the spaces
where light-years expand like arrows
and the planets
are born
of the magic substances of pain—

numbers—root and all
plucked out of murderers' brains
and part already
of the heavenly cycle's
path of blue veins.

Greise

Da,
in den Falten dieses Sterns,
zugedeckt mit einem Fetzen Nacht,
stehen sie, und warten Gott ab.
Ihr Mund hat ein Dorn verschlossen,
ihre Sprache ist an ihre Augen verlorengegangen,
die reden wie Brunnen
darin ein Leichnam ertrunken ist.
O die Alten,
die ihre verbrannte Nachfolge in den Augen tragen
als einzigen Besitz.

Old men

There
in the folds of this star
covered with tatters of night
they stand and wait for God.
A thorn has closed their mouths,
they speak only with their eyes,
they speak like a well
in which a corpse has drowned.
O the old men
who carry their burnt succession in their eyes
as their sole possession.

Welt, frage nicht die Todentrissenen

Welt, frage nicht die Todentrissenen
wohin sie gehen,
sie gehen immer ihrem Grabe zu.
Das Pflaster der fremden Stadt
war nicht für die Musik von Flüchtlingsschritten gelegt
worden—
Die Fenster der Häuser, die eine Erdenzeit spiegeln
mit den wandernden Gabentischen der Bilderbuchhimmel—
wurden nicht für Augen geschliffen
die den Schrecken an seiner Quelle tranken.
Welt, die Falte ihres Lächelns hat ihnen ein starkes Eisen
ausgebrannt;
sie möchten so gerne zu dir kommen
um deiner Schönheit wegen,
aber wer heimatlos ist, dem welken alle Wege
wie Schnittblumen hin—

Aber, es ist uns in der Fremde
eine Freundin geworden: die Abendsonne.
Eingesegnet von ihrem Marterlicht
sind wir geladen zu ihr zu kommen mit unserer Trauer,
die neben uns geht:
Ein Psalm der Nacht.

World, do not ask those snatched from death

World, do not ask those snatched from death
where they are going,
they are always going to their graves.
The pavements of the foreign city
were not laid for the music of fugitive footsteps—
The windows of the houses that reflect a lifetime
of shifting tables heaped with gifts from a picture-book
heaven—
were not cut for eyes
which drank terror at its source.
World, a strong iron has cauterized the wrinkle of their
smile;
they would like to come to you
because of your beauty,
but for the homeless all ways wither
like cut flowers—

But we have found a friend
in exile: the evening sun.
Blessed by its suffering light
we are bidden to come to it with our sorrow
which walks beside us:
A psalm of night.

Auf den Landstrassen der Erde

Auf den Landstrassen der Erde
liegen die Kinder
mit den Wurzeln
aus der Muttererde gerissen.
Das Licht der erloschenen Liebe
ist ihrer Hand entfallen
deren Leere sich mit Wind füllt.

Wenn der Vater aller Waisen,
der Abend, mit ihnen
aus allen Wunden blutet
und ihre zitternden Schatten
die herzzerreissende Angst
ihrer Leiber abmalen—
fallen sie plötzlich hinab in die Nacht
wie in den Tod.

Aber im Schmerzgebirge der Morgendämmerung
sterben ihnen Vater und Mutter
wieder und immer wieder.

The children lie

The children lie
on all the roads of earth
torn by the roots
from mother earth.
The light of extinguished love
has fallen from their hands,
wind fills the empty hands.

When evening, father
of all orphans, bleeds
with them from all wounds
and their trembling shadows
mimic the heartbreaking fear
of their bodies—
they plunge suddenly into night
as though into death.

But at dawn in the hills of pain
they see their fathers and mothers
dying again and again.

O die Heimatlosen Farben des Abendhimmels!

O die Heimatlosen Farben des Abendhimmels!
O die Blüten des Sterbens in den Wolken
wie der Neugeborenen Verbleichen!

O der Schwalben Rätselfragen
an das Geheimnis—
der Möven entmenschter Schrei
aus der Schöpfungszeit—

Woher wir Übriggebliebenen aus Sternverdunkelung?
Woher wir mit dem Licht über dem Haupte
dessen Schatten Tod uns anmalt?

Die Zeit rauscht von unserem Heimweh
wie eine Muschel

und das Feuer in der Tiefe der Erde
weiss schon um unseren Zerfall—

O the homeless colors of the evening sky!

O the homeless colors of the evening sky!
O the blossoms of death in the clouds
like the pale dying of the newly born!

O the riddles that the swallows
ask the mystery—
the inhuman cry of the gulls
from the day of creation—

Whence we survivors of the stars' darkening?
Whence we with the light above our heads
whose shadow death paints on us?

Time roars with our longing for home
like a seashell

and the fire in the depths of the earth
already knows of our ruin—

Nun hat Abraham die Wurzel der Winde gefasst

Nun hat Abraham die Wurzel der Winde gefasst
denn heimkehren wird Israel aus der Zerstreuung.

Eingesammelt hat es Wunden und Martern
auf den Höfen der Welt,
abgeweint alle verschlossenen Türen.

Seine Alten, den Erdenkleidern fast entwachsen
und wie Meerpflanzen die Glieder streckend,

einbalsamiert im Salze der Verzweiflung
und die Klagemauer Nacht im Arm—
werden noch einen kleinen Schlaf tun—

Aber die Jungen haben die Sehnsuchtsfahne entfaltet,
denn ein Acker will von ihnen geliebt werden
und eine Wüste getränkt

und nach der Sonnenseite Gott
sollen die Häuser gebaut werden

und der Abend hat wieder das veilchenscheue Wort,
das nur in der Heimat so blau bereitet wird:
Gute Nacht!

Now Abraham has seized the root of the winds

Now Abraham has seized the root of the winds
for home shall Israel come from the dispersion.

It has gathered wounds and afflictions
in the courtyards of the world,
has bathed all locked doors with its tears.

Its elders, having almost outgrown their earthly garb
and extending their limbs like sea plants,

embalmed in the salt of despair
and the wailing wall night in their arms—
will sleep just a spell longer—

But youth has unfurled its flag of longing,
for a field yearns to be loved by them
and a desert watered

and the house shall be built
to face the sun: God

and evening again has the violet-shy word
that only grows so blue in the homeland:
Good night!

Du sitzt am Fenster

Du sitzt am Fenster
und es schneit—
dein Haar ist weiss
und deine Hände—
aber in den beiden Spiegeln
deines weissen Gesichts
hat sich der Sommer erhalten:
Land, für die ins Unsichtbare erhobenen Wiesen—
Tränke, für Schattenrehe zur Nacht.

Aber klagend sinke ich in deine Weisse,
deinen Schnee—
aus dem sich das Leben so leise entfernt
wie nach einem zu Ende gesprochenen Gebet—

O einzuschlafen in deinem Schnee
mit allem Leid im Feueratem der Welt.

Während die zarten Linien deines Hauptes
schon fortsinken in Meeresnacht
zu neuer Geburt.

You sit by the window

You sit by the window
and it is snowing—
your hair is white
and your hands—
but in both mirrors
of your white face
summer has been maintained:
Land for meadows raised into the invisible—
potions for shadow deer at night.

But mourning I sink into your whiteness,
your snow—
which life leaves ever so quietly
as after a prayer spoken to the end—

O to fall asleep in your snow
with all my grief in the fiery breath of the world.

While the delicate lines on your brow
drown already in the ocean of night
for a new birth.

Wenn der Tag leer wird

Wenn der Tag leer wird
in der Dämmerung,
wenn die bilderlose Zeit beginnt,
die einsamen Stimmen sich verbinden–
die Tiere nichts als Jagende sind
oder gejagt–
die Blumen nur noch Duft–
wenn alles namenlos wird wie am Anfang–
gehst du unter die Katakomben der Zeit,
die sich auftun denen, die nahe am Ende sind–
dort wo die Herzkeime wachsen–
in die dunkle Innerlichkeit hinab
sinkst du–
schon am Tode vorbei
der nur ein windiger Durchgang ist–
und schlägst frierend vom Ausgang
deine Augen auf
in denen schon ein neuer Stern
seinen Abglanz gelassen hat–

When day grows empty

When day grows empty
at dusk,
when the imageless time begins,
the lonely voices combine—
the animals are hunters only
or hunted—
the flowers mere fragrance—
when everything becomes nameless as at the beginning—
then you go beneath the catacombs of time
that open for those nearing the end—
there where the heart has its inception—
down into dark inwardness
you sink—
already past death
that is only a windy passage—
and freezing with exit
you open your eyes
in which a new star
already has left its reflection—

Am Abend weitet sich dein Blick

Am Abend weitet sich dein Blick
sieht über Mitternacht hinaus—
doppelt bin ich vor dir—
grüne Knospe, die aus vertrocknetem Kelchblatt steigt,
in dem Zimmer darin wir zwei Welten angehören.
Du reichst auch schon weit über die Toten,
die hiesigen.
Weisst um das Aufgeblühte
aus der rätselumrindeten Erde.

Wie im Mutterleib das Ungeborene
mit dem Urlicht auf dem Haupte
randlos sieht
von Stern zu Stern—
So fliesst Ende zum Anfang
wie ein Schwanenschrei.
Wir sind in einem Krankenzimmer.
Aber die Nacht gehört den Engeln!

In the evening your vision widens

In the evening your vision widens
looks out beyond midnight—
twofold I stand before you—
green bud rising out of dried-up sepal,
in the room where we are of two worlds.
You too already extend far beyond the dead,
those who are here,
and know of what has flowered
out of the earth with its bark of enigma.

As in the womb the unborn
with the primordial light on its brow
has the rimless view
from star to star—
So ending flows to beginning
like the cry of a swan.
We are in a sickroom.
But the night belongs to the angels.

Wohin O wohin

Wohin O wohin
du Weltall der Sehnsucht
das in der Raupe schon dunkel verzaubert
die Flügel spannt,
mit den Flossen der Fische
immer den Anfang beschreibt
in Wassertiefen, die
ein einziges Herz
ausmessen kann mit dem Senkblei
der Trauer.
Wohin o wohin
du Weltall der Sehnsucht
mit der Träume verlorenen Erdreichen
und der gesprengten Blutbahn des Leibes;
während die Seele zusammengefaltet wartet
auf ihre Neugeburt
unter dem Eis der Todesmaske.

Whither O whither

Whither O whither
you universe of longing
spreading your wings in the chrysalis
already darkly enchanted,
always describing the beginning
with the fins of fishes
in the watery depths which
a single heart
can sound with the plummet
of sorrow.
Whither O whither
you universe of longing
with the dreams of lost earths
and the burst vein of the body;
while the soul, folded, waits
to be born again
under the ice of the death mask.

Schmetterling

Welch schönes Jenseits
ist in deinen Staub gemalt.
Durch den Flammenkern der Erde,
durch ihre steinerne Schale
wurdest du gereicht,
Abschiedswebe in der Vergänglichkeiten Mass.

Schmetterling
aller Wesen gute Nacht!
Die Gewichte von Leben und Tod
senken sich mit deinen Flügeln
auf die Rose nieder
die mit dem heimwärts reifenden Licht welkt.

Welch schönes Jenseits
ist in deinen Staub gemalt.
Welch Königszeichen
im Geheimnis der Luft.

Butterfly

What lovely aftermath
is painted in your dust.
You were led through the flaming
core of earth,
through its stony shell,
webs of farewell in the transient measure.

Butterfly
blessed night of all beings!
The weights of life and death
sink down with your wings
on the rose
which withers with the light ripening homewards.

What lovely aftermath
is painted in your dust.
What royal sign
in the secret of the air.

Völker der Erde

Völker der Erde
ihr, die ihr euch mit der Kraft der unbekannten
Gestirne umwickelt wie Garnrollen,
die ihr näht und wieder auftrennt das Genähte,
die ihr in die Sprachverwirrung steigt
wie in Bienenkörbe,
um im Süssen zu stechen
und gestochen zu werden—

Völker der Erde,
zerstöret nicht das Weltall der Worte,
zerschneidet nicht mit den Messern des Hasses
den Laut, der mit dem Atem zugleich geboren wurde.

Völker der Erde,
O dass nicht Einer Tod meine, wenn er Leben sagt—
und nicht Einer Blut, wenn er Wiege spricht—

Völker der Erde,
lasset die Worte an ihrer Quelle,
denn sie sind es, die die Horizonte
in die wahren Himmel rücken können
und mit ihrer abgewandten Seite
wie eine Maske dahinter die Nacht gähnt
die Sterne gebären helfen—

Peoples of the earth

Peoples of the earth,
you who swathe yourselves with the force of the unknown
constellations as with rolls of thread,
you who sew and sever what is sewn,
you who enter the tangle of tongues
as into beehives,
to sting the sweetness
and be stung—

Peoples of the earth,
do not destroy the universe of words,
let not the knife of hatred lacerate
the sound born together with the first breath.

Peoples of the earth,
O that no one mean death when he says life—
and not blood when he speaks cradle—

Peoples of the earth,
leave the words at their source,
for it is they that can nudge
the horizons into the true heaven
and that, with night gaping behind
their averted side, as behind a mask,
help give birth to the stars—

Wir üben heute schon den Tod von morgen

Wir üben heute schon den Tod von morgen
wo noch das alte Sterben in uns welkt–
O Angst der Menschheit nicht zu überstehn–

O Todgewöhnung bis hinein in Träume
wo Nachtgerüst in schwarze Scherben fällt
und beinern Mond in den Ruinen leuchtet–

O Angst der Menschheit nicht zu überstehn–

Wo sind die sanften Rutengänger
Ruhe-Engel, die den verborgnen Quell
uns angerührt, der von der Müdigkeit
zum Sterben rinnt?

We rehearse tomorrow's death even today

We rehearse tomorrow's death even today
while the old dying still wilts within us—
O humanity's dread not to endure—

O death-accustoming down into dreams
where night scaffolding breaks into black fragments
and moon glows like bones on the ruins—

O humanity's dread not to endure—

Where are you, gentle dowsers,
peace angels that used to touch
the hidden source for us
that flows from weariness
into death.

And No One Knows How to Go On

Das ist der Flüchtlinge Planetenstunde

Das ist der Flüchtlinge Planetenstunde.
Das ist der Flüchtlinge reissende Flucht
in die Fallsucht, den Tod!

Das ist der Sternfall aus magischer Verhaftung
der Schwelle, des Herdes, des Brots.

Das ist der schwarze Apfel der Erkenntnis,
die Angst! Erloschene Liebessonne
die raucht! Das ist die Blume der Eile,
schweissbetropft! Das sind die Jäger
aus Nichts, nur aus Flucht.

Das sind Gejagte, die ihre tödlichen Verstecke
in die Gräber tragen.

Das ist der Sand, erschrocken
mit Girlanden des Abschieds.
Das ist der Erde Vorstoss ins Freie,
ihr stockender Atem
in der Demut der Luft.

That is the fugitives' planetary hour

That is the fugitives' planetary hour.
That is the fugitives' rending flight
into epilepsy, death!

That is the star's fall from its magic fastness
in the threshold, bread and hearth.

That is the black apple of knowledge:
Fear! Extinguished sun of love
that smokes! That is the flower of haste
sweat-soaked! Those are the hunters
of nothingness, only of flight.

Those are the hunted who carry their deadly shelters
with them into their grave.

That is the sand, startled
with garlands of parting.
That is the earth's thrust into freedom,
its halting breath
in the humble air.

Einen Akkord spielen Ebbe und Flut

Einen Akkord spielen Ebbe und Flut,
Jäger und Gejagtes.
Mit vielen Händen
wird Greifen und Befestigung versucht,
Blut ist der Faden.

Finger weisen Aufstellungen,
Körperteile werden eingesetzt
in sterbende Zeichnungen.

Strategie,
Geruch des Leidens—

Glieder auf dem Wege zum Staub
und die Gischt der Sehnsucht
über den Wassern.

Ebb and flood strike a chord

Ebb and flood strike a chord,
hunter and hunted.
Many hands seek to grasp
and strengthen,
blood is the thread.

Fingers point out formations,
body parts are deployed
in dying delineations.

Strategy,
smell of suffering—

Limbs on the road to dust
and the foam of longing
over the waters.

Wer weiss, wo die Sterne stehn

Wer weiss, wo die Sterne stehn
in des Schöpfers Herrlichkeitsordnung
und wo der Friede beginnt
und ob in der Tragödie der Erde
die blutig gerissene Kieme des Fisches
bestimmt ist,
das Sternbild *Marter*
mit seinem Rubinrot zu ergänzen,
den ersten Buchstaben
der wortlosen Sprache zu schreiben—

Wohl besitzt Liebe den Blick,
der durch Gebeine fährt wie ein Blitz
und begleitet die Toten
über den Atemzug hinaus—

aber wo die Abgelösten
ihren Reichtum hinlegen,
ist unbekannt.

Himbeeren verraten sich im schwärzesten Wald
durch ihren Duft,
aber der Toten abgelegte Seelenlast
verrät sich keinem Suchen—
und kann doch beflügelt
zwischen Beton oder Atomen zittern
oder immer da,
wo eine Stelle für Herzklopfen
ausgelassen war.

Who knows where the stars stand

Who knows where the stars stand
in the creator's order of glory
and where peace begins
and if in the tragedy of earth
the torn bloody gill of the fish
is intended
to supplement with its ruby red
the constellation of *Torment,*
to write the first letter
of the wordless language—

True, love has the look
which strikes through bones like lightning
and accompanies the dead
beyond the final breath—

but where the superseded
leave their fortune
is unknown.

Raspberries betray their presence by their scent
in the darkest wood,
but no search will reveal
the agonies the dead have laid aside
and which can still quicken and tremble
between atoms and concrete
or there, always,
where a place has been left
for heartbeats.

Erde, Planetengreis, du saugst an meinem Fuss

Erde, Planetengreis, du saugst an meinem Fuss,
der fliegen will,
o König Lear mit der Einsamkeit im Arme.

Nach innen weinst du mit den Meeresaugen
die Leidenstrümmer
in die Seelenwelt.

Auf deiner Silberlocken Jahrmillionen
den Erdrauchkranz, Wahnsinn gestirnt
im Brandgeruch.

Und deine Kinder,
die schon deinen Todesschatten werfen,
da du dich drehst und drehst
auf deiner Sternenstelle,
Milchstrassenbettler
mit dem Wind als Blindenhund.

Earth, old man of the planets, you suck at my foot

Earth, old man of the planets, you suck at my foot
which wants to fly,
O King Lear embracing loneliness.

With sea-eyes you weep
the rubble of suffering
into realms of the soul within.

On the millennia of your silver locks
the wreathed smoke of earth, madness crowned
in the smell of burning.

And your children
who already cast the shadow of your death,
as you turn and turn
in your place among the stars,
beggar of the Milky Way
with the wind as guide-dog.

In einer Landschaft aus Musik

In einer Landschaft aus Musik,
in einer Sprache nur aus Licht,
in einer Glorie,
die das Blut
sich mit der Sehnsucht Zunge angezündet,

dort wo die Häute,
Augen, Horizonte,
wo Hand und Fuss
schon ohne Zeichen sind,

dort wo des Sandelbaumes Duft
schon holzlos schwebt
und Atem baut an jenem Raume weiter,
der nur aus übertretnen Schwellen ist—

Hier wo ein rotes Abendtuch
den Stier des Lebens reizt
bis in den Tod,

hier liegt mein Schatten,
eine Hand der Nacht,

die mit des schwarzen Jägers Jagegeist
des Blutes roten Vogel
angeschossen hat.

In a landscape of music

In a landscape of music,
in a language only of light,
in an aureole
that blood has lighted
with its yearning tongue,

where skin,
eyes, horizons,
where hand and foot
already are without token,

where the sandal tree's fragrance
hovers woodless in the air
and breath builds on to that room
consisting only of thresholds that have been surpassed—

Here where a red evening muleta
lures the bull of life
to his death,

here lies my shadow,
a hand of the night,

that has wounded the red bird of blood
with the black hunter's hunting spirit.

Hier und da ist die Laterne der Barmherzigkeit

Hier und da ist die Laterne der Barmherzigkeit
zu den Fischen zu stellen,
wo der Angelhaken geschluckt
oder das Ersticken geübt wird.

Dort ist das Gestirn der Qualen
erlösungsreif geworden.

Oder dahin,
wo Liebende sich wehe tun,
Liebende,
die doch immer nahe am Sterben sind.

Here and there the lantern of compassion

Here and there the lantern of compassion
can be shown to the fish,
where the fishhook is swallowed
or suffocation practiced.

There the star of anguish
has grown ripe for redemption.

Or there,
where lovers hurt each other,
Lovers,
who are always close to dying.

In der blauen Ferne

In der blauen Ferne,
wo die rote Apfelbaumallee wandert
mit himmelbesteigenden Wurzelfüssen,
wird die Sehnsucht destilliert
für Alle die im Tale leben.

Die Sonne, am Wegesrand liegend
mit Zauberstäben,
gebietet Halt den Reisenden.

Die bleiben stehn
im gläsernen Albtraum,
während die Grille fein kratzt
am Unsichtbaren

und der Stein seinen Staub
tanzend in Musik verwandelt.

In the blue distance

In the blue distance
where the red row of apple trees wanders
—rooted feet climbing the sky—
the longing is distilled
for all those who live in the valley.

The sun, lying by the roadside
with magic wands,
commands the travelers to halt.

They stand still
in the glassy nightmare
while the cricket scratches softly
at the invisible

and the stone dancing
changes its dust to music.

Und wir, die ziehen

Und wir, die ziehen
über alle Blätter der Windrose hinweg
schweres Erbe in die Fernen.

Ich hier,
wo Erde schon angesichtslos wird
der Pol,
des Todes weisser Bienensaug
in der Stille weisse Blätter fällt

der Elch,
lugend durch blaue Vorhänge,
blass gebrütetes Sonnenei
zwischen seinen Schaufeln trägt—

Hier, wo Meereszeit
sich vermummt mit Eisbergmasken
unter letzten Sterns
gefrorenem Wundmal

hier an dieser Stelle
aussetzte ich die Koralle,
die blutende,
deiner Botschaft.

And we who move away

And we who move away
beyond all leaves of the windrose
heavy inheritance into the distance.

Myself here,
where earth is losing its lineaments
the Pole,
death's white dead nettle
falls in the stillness of white leaves

the elk,
peering through blue curtains,
between his antlers bears
a sun-egg hatched pale—

Here, where ocean time
camouflages itself with iceberg masks
under the last star's
frozen stigma

here at this place
I expose the coral,
the one that bleeds
with your message.

Bereit sind alle Länder aufzustehn

Bereit sind alle Länder aufzustehn
von der Landkarte.
Abzuschütteln ihre Sternenhaut
die blauen Bündel ihrer Meere
auf dem Rücken zu knüpfen
ihre Berge mit den Feuerwurzeln
als Mützen auf die rauchenden Haare zu setzen.

Bereit das letzte Schwermutgewicht
im Koffer zu tragen, diese Schmetterlingspuppe,
auf deren Flügeln sie die Reise einmal
beenden werden.

All lands are ready to rise

All lands are ready to rise
from the map.
To shake off their skin of stars
to tie the blue bundles of their seas
on their backs
to set their mountains with fiery roots
as caps on their smoking hair.

Ready to carry the last weight
of melancholy in a suitcase, this chrysalis
on the wings of which they will one day
end the journey.

Vergessenheit! Haut

Vergessenheit! Haut,
daraus Neugeborenes gewickelt wird
und Sterbelaken,
das die weiss schlafenden Heimholer
wieder ausleihen.

Zuweilen auf letzter Landzunge
des Blutes
das Nebelhorn ertönt
und der ertrunkene Matrose singt

oder auf sandigem Landweg
Spuren laufen
aus Sehnsuchtslabarynthen
wie zerbrochene Schneckenhäuser,
Leere auf dem Rücken tragend—

Hinter der Dämmerung
Amselmusik

Tote tanzen
Blütenhalme des Windes—

Oblivion! Skin

Oblivion! Skin
out of which what is newborn is wound
and sheets for the dying
that the white sleepers
who bring it home
lend out again.

At times on the blood's
last spit of land
the foghorn resounds
and the drowned sailor sings

or on a sandy country path
trails of footsteps run
from labyrinths of longing
like broken snail shells
bearing emptiness on their back—

Behind the dusk
music of blackbirds

The dead dance
flower stalks of the wind—

Verwunschen ist alles zur Hälfte

Verwunschen ist alles zur Hälfte.
Abwärts wandert das Licht
ins Hintergründige–
kein Messer schuppt die Nacht.

Trost wohnt weit
hinter der Narbe aus Heimweh.
Vielleicht,
wo anderes Grün mit Zungen redet
und die Meere sich zeitlos überlassen.

Ausfährt im Sterben
der Rätsel Kometenschweif,
leuchtet,
wenn die Seele
sich heimtastet an seinem Geländer.

Wohl weiden Kühe im Vordergrund,
Klee duftet Honig
und der Schritt begräbt Engelvergessenes.

In der Stadt knattert Erwachen,
aber über Brücken gehn,
ist nur, um einen Arbeitsplatz zu erreichen.

Auf der Strasse rasselt Milch in Kannen
für alle,
die den Tod als letzten Geschmack saugen.

Bewitched is half of everything

Bewitched is half of everything.
Downward wanders the light
into obscurities—
no knife unscales the night.

Solace lives far
behind the homesickness scar.
Perhaps
where a different green speaks with tongues
and the seas abandon themselves timelessly.

The enigmas' trail of comets
erupts in death,
glows
when the soul
gropes home along its railing.

True, cows graze in the foreground,
clover is fragrant with honey
and the step buries what angels forgot.

Awakening clangs in the city
but to cross bridges
is only to reach a job.

Milk rattles in cans on the street
for all who imbibe death as their last taste.

Die Lachmöwe über dem Wasser
hat noch einen Tropfen Wahnsinn
vom Hinter-dem-Wald-Leben
behalten.

Melusine,
dein landloser Teil
ist in unserer Träne geborgen.

The laughing gull above the water
still has a drop of madness
from living-in-the-backwoods.

Melusine,
your landless part
is preserved in our tear.

Da schrieb der Schreiber des Sohar

Da schrieb der Schreiber des Sohar
und öffnete der Worte Adernetz
und führte Blut von den Gestirnen ein,
die kreisten unsichtbar, und nur
von Sehnsucht angezündet.

Des Alphabetes Leiche hob sich aus dem Grab,
Buchstabenengel, uraltes Kristall,
mit Wassertropfen von der Schöpfung eingeschlossen,
die sangen—und man sah durch sie
Rubin und Hyazinth und Lapis schimmern,
als Stein noch weich war
und wie Blumen ausgesät.

Und, schwarzer Tiger, brüllte auf
die Nacht; und wälzte sich
und blutete mit Funken
die Wunde Tag.

Das Licht war schon ein Mund der schwieg,
nur eine Aura noch den Seelengott verriet.

Then wrote the scribe of The Sohar

Then wrote the scribe of *The Sohar*
opening the words' mesh of veins
instilling blood from stars
which circled, invisible, and ignited
only by yearning.

The alphabet's corpse rose from the grave,
alphabet angel, ancient crystal,
immured by creation in drops of water
that sang—and through them you saw
glinting lapis, ruby and jacinth,
when stone was still soft
and sown like flowers.

And night, the black tiger,
roared; and there tossed
and bled with sparks
the wound called day.

The light was a mouth that did not speak,
only an aura intimated the soul-god now.

Und wickelt aus, als wärens Linnentücher

Und wickelt aus, als wärens Linnentücher,
darin Geburt und Tod ist eingehüllt,
Buchstabenleib, die Falterpuppe
aus grüner, roter, weisser Finsternis
und wickelt wieder ein in Liebesleiden
wie Mütter tun; denn Leiden ist Versteck fürs Licht.

Doch während er wie Sommer oder Winter handelt,
schwebt schon Ersehntes, sehnsuchtsvoll verwandelt.

And unwraps, as though it were linen sheets

And unwraps, as though it were linen sheets
in which birth and death are swathed,
the alphabet womb, chrysalis
of green and red and white obscurity
and swaddles it again in love-grief
as mothers do; for grief is a hiding place for light.

Yet while like summer he behaves, or winter,
yearned-for things already hover, yearnfully transformed.

Landschaft aus Schreien

In der Nacht, wo Sterben Genähtes zu trennen beginnt,
reisst die Landschaft aus Schreien
den schwarzen Verband auf,

Über Moria, dem Klippenabsturz zu Gott,
schwebt des Opfermessers Fahne
Abrahams Herz-Sohn-Schrei,
am grossen Ohr der Bibel liegt er bewahrt.

O die Hieroglyphen aus Schreien,
an die Tod-Eingangstür gezeichnet.

Wundkorallen aus zerbrochenen Kehlenflöten.

O, o Hände mit Angstpflanzenfinger,
eingegraben in wildbäumende Mähnen Opferblutes—

Schreie, mit zerfetzten Kiefern der Fische verschlossen,
Weheranke der kleinsten Kinder
und der schluckenden Atemschleppe der Greise,

eingerissen in versengtes Azur mit brennenden Schweifen.
Zellen der Gefangenen, der Heiligen,
mit Albtraummuster der Kehlen tapezierte,
fiebernde Hölle in der Hundehütte des Wahnsinns
aus gefesselten Sprüngen—

Landscape of screams

At night when dying proceeds to sever all seams
the landscape of screams
tears open the black bandage,

Above Moria, the falling off cliffs to God,
there hovers the flag of the sacrificial knife
Abraham's scream for the son of his heart,
at the great ear of the Bible it lies preserved.

O hieroglyphs of screams
engraved at the entrance gate to death.

Wounded coral of shattered throat flutes.

O, O hands with finger vines of fear,
dug into wildly rearing manes of sacrificial blood—

Screams, shut tight with the shredded mandibles of fish,
woe tendril of the smallest children
and the gulping train of breath of the very old,

slashed into seared azure with burning tails.
Cells of prisoners, of saints,
tapestried with the nightmare pattern of throats,
seething hell in the doghouse of madness
of shackled leaps—

Dies is die Landschaft aus Schreien!
Himmelfahrt aus Schreien,
empor aus des Leibes Knochengittern,

Pfeile aus Schrein, erlöste
aus blutigen Köchern.

Hiobs Vier-Winde-Schrei
und der Schrei verborgen im Ölberg
wie ein von Ohnmacht übermanntes Insekt im Kristall.

O Messer aus Abendrot, in die Kehlen geworfen,
wo die Schlafbäume blutleckend aus der Erde fahren,
wo die Zeit wegfällt
an den Gerippen in Maidanek und Hiroshima.

Ascheschrei aus blindgequältem Seherauge—

O du blutendes Auge
in der zerfetzten Sonnenfinsternis
zum Gott-Trocknen aufgehängt
im Weltall—

This is the landscape of screams!
Ascension made of screams
out of the bodies grate of bones,

arrows of screams, released
from bloody quivers.

Job's scream to the four winds
and the scream concealed in Mount Olive
like a crystal-bound insect overwhelmed by impotence.

O knife of evening red, flung into the throats
where trees of sleep rear blood-licking from the ground,
where time is shed
from the skeletons in Hiroshima and Maidanek.

Ashen scream from visionary eye tortured blind—

O you bleeding eye
in the tattered eclipse of the sun
hung up to be dried by God
in the cosmos—

Mit Wildhonig

Mit Wildhonig
die Hinterbliebenen
nährten
in frühen Gräbern
einbalsamierten Schlaf
und ausgewanderte Pulse
gossen Dattelwein
in die Bienenwabe
der Geheimnisse.

Im schwarzen Kristall der Nacht
die eingeschlossene Wespe
der ausgetanzten Zeit
im Starrkrampf lag—

Aber du,
aber du,
wie nähre ich dich?

Alle Meilensteine aus Staub
überspringt die Liebe,
wie die geköpfte Sonne
im Schmerz
nur Untergang suchend.

Mit meinem Untergang
nähre ich dich—

With wild honey

With wild honey
the bereaved
fed
embalmed sleep
and departed pulses
in early graves
poured date wine
into the honeycomb
of the mysteries.

In black crystal of night
the trapped wasp
of an outdanced time
lay locked in cramp—

But you,
but you,
how shall I feed you?

Love springs over
all milestones of dust
like the beheaded sun
in pain
seeking only descent.

With my descent
I feed you—

Wieviele Meere im Sande verlaufen

Wieviele Meere im Sande verlaufen,
wieviel Sand hart gebetet im Stein,
wieviel Zeit im Sanghorn der Muscheln
verweint,
wieviel Todverlassenheit
in den Perlenaugen der Fische,
wieviele Morgentrompeten in der Koralle,
wieviel Sternenmuster im Kristall,
wieviel Lachkeime in der Kehle der Möwe,
wieviel Heimwehfäden
auf nächtlichen Gestirnbahnen gefahren,
wieviel fruchtbares Erdreich
für die Wurzel des Wortes:
Du—
hinter allen stürzenden Gittern
der Geheimnisse
Du—

How many oceans have vanished in sand

How many oceans have vanished in sand,
how much sand has been prayed hard in the stone,
how much time has been wept away
in the singing horn of the seashells,
how much mortal abandonment
in the fishes' pearl eyes,
how many morning trumpets in the coral,
how many star patterns in crystal,
how much seed of laughter in the gull's throat,
how many threads of longing for home
have been traversed on the nightly course of the
constellations,
how much fertile earth
for the root of the word:
You—
behind all the crashing screens
of the secrets
You—

O Schwester

O Schwester
wo zeltest du?

Im schwarzen Geflügelhof
lockst du die Küken deines Wahnsinns
fütterst sie gross.

Wunden in die Luft
kräht des Hahnes Trompete—

Wie ein entblösster Vogel
bist du aus dem Nest gefallen
Spaziergänger beäugen
das Schamlose.

Mit dem Albdruckbesen
kehrst du heimattreu
die rauchenden Meteore
vor des Paradieses Flammenpforte
hin und zurück . . .

Dynamit der Ungeduld
stösst dich zu tanzen
auf den schiefen Blitzen der Erleuchtung.

Dein Leib klafft Aussichtspunkte
Verlorenes Pyramidenmass
holst du herein

O sister

O sister,
where do you pitch your tent?

In the black chicken-run
you call the brood of your madness
and rear them.

The cock's trumpet
crows wounds into the air–

You have fallen from the nest
like a naked bird
passers-by eye
that brazenness.

True to your native land
you sweep the roaring meteors
back and forth with a nightmare broom
before the flaming gates of paradise . . .

Dynamite of impatience
pushes you out to dance
on the tilted flashes of inspiration.

Your body gapes points of view
you recover the lost
dimensions of the pyramids

Vögel
die auf deinem Augenast sitzen
zwitschern dir die blühende Geometrie
einer Sternenzeichnung.

In deiner Hand
verpuppten Rätselmoos
wickelt sich die Nacht aus

bis du den flügelatmenden Morgenfalter hältst
zuckend—
zuckend—
mit einem Schrei
trinkst du sein Blut.

Birds
sitting in the branches of your eye
twitter to you the blossoming geometry
of a map of stars.

Night unfolds
a chrysalis of enigmatic moss
in your hand

until you hold the wing-breathing butterfly of morning
quivering—
quivering—
with a cry
you drink its blood.

In zweideutiger Berufung

In zweideutiger Berufung
der getretne Wurm des Lebens
windet sich an Übergängen,
streckt weiche Fühler
durch des Schlafes Laubhütte—

Adern öffnen sich im wundenlosen Nichts
der Meerfahrenden,
singend in der Sarabande
der Sterne—
Die Zeit malt ihr Ende
mit einem blitzenden Widdergehörn—

In ambiguous calling

In ambiguous calling
the trampled worm of life
writhes on gradations,
extends soft feelers
through the bower of sleep—

Veins open in the unwounded nothingness
of seafarers
singing in the saraband
of stars—
Time paints its end
with a flashing ram's horn—

Salzige Zungen aus Meer

Salzige Zungen aus Meer
lecken an den Perlen unserer Krankheit—
Die Rose am Horizont,
nicht aus Staub,
aber aus Nacht,
sinkt in deine Geburt—
Hier im Sand
ihre schwarz
mit Zeit umwickelte Chiffre
wächst wie Haar
noch im Tod—

Salty ocean tongues

Salty ocean tongues
lick at the pearls of our sickness—
The rose on the horizon,
not of dust
but of night,
sinks into your birth—
Here in the sand
its black cipher
swathed in time
grows, hair-like,
even in death—

Flight and Metamorphosis

In der Flucht

In der Flucht
welch grosser Empfang
unterwegs—

Eingehüllt
in der Winde Tuch
Füsse im Gebet des Sandes
der niemals Amen sagen kann
denn er muss
von der Flosse in den Flügel
und weiter—

Der kranke Schmetterling
weiss bald wieder vom Meer—
Dieser Stein
mit der Inschrift der Fliege
hat sich mir in die Hand gegeben—

An Stelle von Heimat
halte ich die Verwandlungen der Welt—

Fleeing

Fleeing,
what a great reception
on the way—

Wrapped
in the wind's shawl
feet in the prayer of sand
which can never say amen
compelled
from fin to wing
and further—

The sick butterfly
will soon learn again of the sea—
This stone
with the fly's inscription
gave itself into my hand—

I hold instead of a homeland
the metamorphoses of the world—

Tänzerin

Tänzerin
bräutlich
aus Blindenraum
empfängst du
ferner Schöpfungstage
spriessende Sehnsucht—

Mit deines Leibes Musikstrassen
weidest du die Luft ab
dort
wo der Erdball
neuen Eingang sucht
zur Geburt.

Durch
Nachtlava
wie leise sich lösende
Augenlider
blinzelt der Schöpfungsvulkane
Erstlingsschrei.

Im Gezweige deiner Glieder
bauen die Ahnungen
ihre zwitschernden Nester.

Dancer

Dancer
like a bride
you conceive
from blind space
the sprouting longing
of distant days of creation—

With the streets of your body's music
you feed upon the air
there
where the globe of earth
seeks new access
to birth.

Through
night-lava
like
eyelids opening gently
the first cry of the creative volcano
blinks.

In the branches of your limbs
the premonitions
build their twittering nests.

Wie eine Melkerin
in der Dämmerung
ziehen deine Fingerspitzen
an den verborgenen Quellen
des Lichtes
bis du durchstochen von der
Marter des Abends
dem Mond deine Augen
zur Nachtwache auslieferst.

Tänzerin
kreissende Wöchnerin
du allein
trägst an verborgener Nabelschnur
an deinem Leib
den Gott vererbten Zwillingsschmuck
von Tod und Geburt.

Like a milkmaid
at dusk
your fingertips pull
at the hidden sources
of light
until you, pierced by the
torment of evening,
surrender your eyes
to the moon for her vigil.

Dancer
woman in childbirth
you alone
carry on the hidden navel-string
of your body
the identical god-given jewels
of death and birth.

Sieh doch

Sieh doch
sieh doch
der Mensch bricht aus
mitten auf dem Marktplatz
hörst du seine Pulse schlagen
und die grosse Stadt
gegürtet um seinen Leib
auf Gummirädern–
denn das Schicksal
hat das Rad der Zeit
vermummt–
hebt sich
an seinen Atemzügen.

Gläserne Auslagen
zerbrochene Rabenaugen
verfunkeln
schwarz flaggen die Schornsteine
das Grab der Luft.

Aber der Mensch
hat *Ah* gesagt
und steigt
eine grade Kerze
in die Nacht.

But look

But look
but look
man breaks out
in the middle of the marketplace
can you hear his pulses beating
and the great city
on rubber tires
girded about his body—
for fate
has muffled
the wheel of time—
lifts itself
on the rhythm of his breathing.

Glassy displays
broken raven-eyes
sparkle
the chimneys fly black flags
at the grave of air.

But man
has said *Ah*
and climbs
a straight candle
into the night.

Einer

Einer
wird den Ball
aus der Hand der furchtbar
Spielenden nehmen.

Sterne
haben ihr eigenes Feuergesetz
und ihre Fruchtbarkeit
ist das Licht
und Schnitter und Ernteleute
sind nicht von hier.

Weit draussen
sind ihre Speicher gelagert
auch Stroh
hat einen Augenblick Leuchtkraft
bemalt Einsamkeit.

Einer wird kommen
und ihnen das Grün der Frühlingsknospe
an den Gebetmantel nähen
und als Zeichen gesetzt
an die Stirn des Jahrhunderts
die Seidenlocke des Kindes.

Someone

Someone
will take the ball
from the hands that play
the game of terror.

Stars
have their own law of fire
and their fertility
is the light
and reapers and harvesters
are not native here.

Far off
stand their granaries
straw too
has a momentary power of illumination
painting loneliness.

Someone will come
and sew the green of the spring bud
on their prayer shawl
and set the child's silken curl
as a sign
on the brow of the century.

Hier ist
Amen zu sagen
diese Krönung der Worte die
ins Verborgene zieht
und
Frieden
du grosses Augenlid
das alle Unruhe verschliesst
mit deinem himmlischen Wimpernkranz

Du leiseste aller Geburten.

Here Amen
must be said
this crowning of words
which moves into hiding
and
peace
you great eyelid
closing on all unrest
your heavenly wreath of lashes

You most gentle of all births.

Und überall

Und überall
der Mensch in der Sonne
den schwarzen Aderlass Schuld
werfend in den Sand—
und nur im Schlaf
dem tränenlosen Versteck
mit dem lodernden Pfeil des Heimwehs
fahrend aus dem Köcher der Haut—

Aber hier
immer nur Buchstaben
die ritzen das Auge
sind aber lange schon
unnütze Weisheitszähne geworden
Reste eines entschlummerten Zeitalters.

And everywhere

And everywhere
mankind in the sun
flinging black bloodletting, guilt,
into the sand—
and only in sleep
the tearless hiding place
with the blazing arrow of homesickness
flying out of the quiver of skin—

But here
nothing but letters
that scratch the eye
but became useless wisdom teeth
long ago
remains of an age passed away.

Jetzt aber
der Wettercherub
knotet
das Vier-Winde-Tuch
nicht um Erdbeeren zu sammeln
in den Wäldern der Sprache
sondern
die Trompete veränderlich anzublasen
im Dunkel
denn nicht kann Sicherheit sein
im fliegenden Staub
und nur das Kopftuch aus Wind
eine bewegliche Krone
zeigt noch züngelnd
mit Unruhgestirnen geschmückt
den Lauf der Welt an—

But now
the weather cherub
is tying
the four winds' scarf
not to pick strawberries
in the forest of tongues
but to blow the trumpet changeably
in the dark
for certainty can be none
in the flying dust
and only the scarf of wind
a movable crown
adorned with restless stars
still darts in and out
and points to the course of the world—

Wie viele

Wie viele
ertrunkene Zeiten
im rauschenden Schlepptau des Kinderschlafes
steigen ein auf hoher See
in die duftende Kajüte
spielend auf mondenen Gebeinen der Toten
wenn die Jungfrau mit der nachtgesprenkelten
Sonnenlimone
hineinblendet
aus Schiffsuntergang.

Hilflos
auf und zu
schlagen der Augenblicke Schmetterlingstüren
unverschliessbar
für die goldenen Lanzen
die mordbrennenden
in das blutende Schlachtfeld der Kinderangst.

Was für Umwege sind zu gehen
für Herzschritte
bevor endlich
das Erinnerungsboot
das tagfahrende
erreicht ist—

How many

How many
drowned ages
in the roaring towline of childhood sleep
enter the fragrant cabin
on the high sea
playing over the moon-colored bones of the dead
when the virgin with the night-flecked
sun citrus
sends blinding rays
out of shipwreck.

Helplessly
open and shut
beat the moment's butterfly doors
always pervious
to the golden lances
that sear murderously
into the bleeding battleground of childhood fear.

What detours
must heart steps take
before the memory boat
that travels by day
finally has been reached—

Wie viele traumumspülte Grenzen der Erde
sind auszuziehen
bis Musik kommt
von einem fremden Gestirn—

Wie viele todkranke Eroberungen
müssen sie machen
ehe sie heimkehren
Mondmilch im Munde
in die schreiende Luft
ihrer hellbewimpelten Kinderspielplätze—

How many dream-washed limits of earth
must be drawn out
till music comes
from an alien star—

How many mortally sick conquests
must they make
before coming home
moon-milk in their mouths
into the screaming air
of their brightly pennoned childhood playground—

Kommt einer

Kommt einer
von ferne
mit einer Sprache
die vielleicht die Laute
verschliesst
mit dem Wiehern der Stute
oder
dem Piepen
junger Schwarzamseln
oder
auch wie eine knirschende Säge
die alle Nähe zerschneidet—

Kommt einer
von ferne
mit Bewegungen des Hundes
oder
vielleicht der Ratte
und es ist Winter
so kleide ihn warm
kann auch sein
er hat Feuer unter den Sohlen
(vielleicht ritt er
auf einem Meteor)
so schilt ihn nicht
falls dein Teppich durchlöchert schreit—

Someone comes

Someone comes
from afar
with a language
that perhaps immures
its vowels
in the neighing of a mare
or
the piping
of young blackbirds
or
screeches like a saw
which rives all nearness—

Someone comes
from afar
who moves like a dog
or
perhaps a rat
and it is winter
so clothe him warmly,
or he may have
fire beneath his feet
(perhaps he rode
on a meteor)
so do not scold him
if your carpet screams with holes—

Ein Fremder hat immer
seine Heimat im Arm
wie eine Waise
für die er vielleicht nichts
als ein Grab sucht.

A stranger always has
his homeland in his arms
like an orphan
for which he may be seeking
nothing but a grave.

Weiter

Weiter
weiter
durch das Rauchbild
abgebrannter Liebesmeilen
hin zum Meer
das grollend beisst
seinen Horizontenring in Stücke—

Weiter
weiter
hin zum Schwarzgespann
mit dem Sonnenkopf im Wagen
das auf weisse Mauern steigt
durch den Stacheldraht der Zeit
in das Auge des Gefangenen sinkt
blutbeträuft—
bis der endlich
weiter
weiter
mit dem Schlaf verbrüdert
in die grosse Freiheit läuft—

Schon hat ihn der Traum gefangen
in dem sterngeschlossenen Zirkel . . .

Further

Further
further
through the smoking image
of burnt-down miles of love
on to the sea
that growls and bites
the ring of its horizon into pieces—

Further
further
on to the team of black horses,
with the head of the sun in the wagon,
which climbs white walls
through the barbed wire of time
sinking sprinkled with blood
into the prisoner's eye—
until he finally
further
further
a brother of sleep
runs out into the great freedom—

Already the dream has caught him
in the star-locked circle . . .

Linie wie

Linie wie
lebendiges Haar
gezogen
todnachtgedunkelt
von dir
zu mir.

Gegängelt
ausserhalb
bin ich hinübergeneigt
durstend
das Ende der Fernen zu küssen.

Der Abend
wirft das Sprungbrett
der Nacht über das Rot
verlängert deine Landzunge
und ich setze meinen Fuss zagend
auf die zitternde Saite
des schon begonnenen Todes

Aber so ist die Liebe—

Line like

Line like
living hair
drawn
deathnightobscured
from you
to me.

Reined in
outside
I bend
thirstily
to kiss the end of all distances.

Evening
throws the springboard
of night over the redness
lengthens your promontory
and hesitant I place my foot
on the trembling string
of my death already begun.

But such is love—

Der Schlafwandler

Der Schlafwandler
kreisend auf seinem Stern
an der weissen Feder des Morgens
erwacht—
der Blutfleck darauf erinnerte ihn—
lässt den Mond
erschrocken fallen—
die Schneebeere zerbricht
am schwarzen Achat der Nacht—
traumbesudelt—

Kein reines Weiss auf Erden—

The sleepwalker

The sleepwalker
circling upon his star
is awakened by
the white feather of morning—
the bloodstain on it reminds him—
startled, he drops
the moon—
the snowberry breaks
against the black agate of night
sullied with dream—

No spotless white on this earth—

Weisse Schlange

Weisse Schlange
Polarkreis
Flügel im Granit
rosa Wehmut im Eisblock
Sperrzonen um das Geheimnis
Herzklopfenmeilen aus Entfernung
Windketten hängend am Heimweh
flammende Granate aus Zorn–

Und die Schnecke
mit dem tickenden Gepäck der Gottzeit.

White serpent

White serpent
polar circle
wings in the granite
rose-colored sadness in blocks of ice
frontier zones around the secret
heartthrobbing miles of distance
wind-chains hanging from homesickness
flaming grenade of anger—

And the snail
with the ticking luggage of God's time.

Wie viele Heimatländer

Wie viele Heimatländer
spielen Karten in den Lüften
wenn der Flüchtling durchs Geheimnis geht

wie viel schlafende Musik
im Gehölz der Zweige
wo der Wind einsam
den Geburtenhelfer spielt.

Blitzgeöffnet
sät
Buchstaben-Springwurzelwald
in verschlingende Empfängnis
Gottes erstes Wort.

Schicksal zuckt
in den blutbefahrenen Meridianen einer Hand—

Alles endlos ist
und an Strahlen
einer Ferne aufgehängt—

How many homelands

How many homelands
play cards in the air
when the refugee goes through the mystery

how much sleeping music
in the tangled branches
where wind lonesomely
plays midwife.

Cleft by lightning
alphabet-leaprootforest
sows
God's first word
into devouring reception.

Fate flinches
in the blood-traversed meridians of a hand—

Endless is everything
and suspended
on rays of distance—

Schon

Schon
mit der Mähne des Haares
Fernen entzündend
schon
mit den ausgesetzten
den Fingerspitzen
den Zehen
im Offenen pirschenden
das Weite suchend–

Der Ozeane Salzruf
an der Uferlinie des Leibes

Gräber
verstossen in Vergessenheit
wenn auch Heilkraut für Atemwunden–

An unseren Hautgrenzen
tastend die Toten
im Schauer der Geburten
Auferstehung feiernd

Wortlos gerufen
schifft sich Göttliches ein–

Already

Already
igniting the distances
with the mane of hair
already
seeking open spaces
with the extremities
the fingertips
and toes
that stalk in the outside–

The ocean's salt call
at the body's shoreline

Graves
cast out into oblivion
though healing herb for breath wounds–

At the limits of our skin
grope the dead
in the dread of births
celebrating resurrection

Wordlessly called
the supernal boards the ship–

Hinter den Lippen

Hinter den Lippen
Unsagbares wartet
reisst an den Nabelsträngen
der Worte

Märtyrersterben der Buchstaben
in der Urne des Mundes
geistige Himmelfahrt
aus schneidendem Schmerz—

Aber der Atem der inneren Rede
durch die Klagemauer der Luft
haucht geheimnisentbundene Beichte
sinkt ins Asyl
der Weltenwunde
noch im Untergang
Gott abgelauscht—

Behind the lips

Behind the lips
waits the ineffable
tears at the words'
umbilical cords

Martyrdom of the letters
in the urn of the mouth
spiritual ascension
of incisive pain—

But the breath of the inner speech
through the wailing-wall air
breathes confession delivered of all its secrets
sinks into the asylum
of the world wound
it had gleaned from God
even in its ruin—

Abgewandt

Abgewandt
warte ich auf dich
weit fort von den Lebenden weilst du
oder nahe.

Abgewandt
warte ich auf dich
denn nicht dürfen Freigelassene
mit Schlingen der Sehnsucht
eingefangen werden
noch gekrönt
mit der Krone aus Planetenstaub—

die Liebe ist eine Sandpflanze
die im Feuer dient
und nicht verzehrt wird—

Abgewandt
wartet sie auf dich—

Estranged

Estranged
I wait for you
you linger far from the living
or near.

Estranged
I wait for you
for the liberated
may not be captured
with nooses of longing
nor crowned
with the crown of planetary dust—

love is a flower that grows in sand
which serves in fire
and is not devoured—

Estranged
she waits for you—

Erlöste

Erlöste
aus Schlaf
werden die grossen Dunkelheiten
der Steinkohlenwälder
auffahren
abwerfen
das glitzernde Laub
der Lichterjahre
und ihre Seele aufdecken–

Beter
nackend
aus Blitzen
und Gesang aus Feuer
kniend
stossend
mit Geweihen des Ausser-sich-Seins
wieder an den Klippen des Anfangs
bei der Wogenmütter
Welt einrollender Musik.

Redeemed

Redeemed
from sleep
the great darknesses
of the coal forests
will
leap up
shedding
the glittering leaves
of light-years
and reveal their souls—

Naked
worshipper
of lightning
and song of fire
kneeling
thrusting again
with antlers of being-beside-oneself
at the cliffs of beginning
with the wave-mother's
world-encircling music.

Journey into a Dustless Realm

Wer

Wer
von der Erde kommt
Mond zu berühren
oder
anderes Himmelsmineral das blüht–
angeschossen
von Erinnerung
wird er hoch springen
vom explodierenden Sehnsuchtsstoff
denn
aus bemalter Erdennacht
aufgeflügelt sind seine Gebete
aus täglichen Vernichtungen
suchend die inneren Augenstrassen.

Krater und Trockenmeere
erfüllt von Tränen
durch sternige Stationen reisend
auf der Fahrt ins Staublose.

Whoever

Whoever
leaves the earth
to touch the moon
or
other heavenly minerals that bloom—
wounded
by remembrance
will he leap up
with the exploding stuff of yearning,
for
from painted terrestrial night
his prayers have winged up
out of the daily annihilations
to search for the inward streets of the eyes.

Craters and parched seas
drenched with tears
journeying through starry stations
on their way to a dustless realm.

Überall die Erde
baut an ihren Heimwehkolonien.
Nicht zu landen
auf den Ozeanen des süchtigen Blutes
nur zu wiegen sich
in Lichtmusik aus Ebbe und Flut
nur zu wiegen sich
im Rhythmus des unverwundeten
Ewigkeitszeichen:
Leben—Tod—

Everywhere the earth
is building its homesickness colonies.
Not to land
on the oceans of lustful blood
only to sway
in the light-music of ebb and flood
only to sway
in the rhythm of the unwounded
sign of eternity:
                    Life—Death—

Du

Du
in der Nacht
mit dem Verlernen der Welt Beschäftigte
von weit weit her
dein Finger die Eisgrotte bemalte
mit der singenden Landkarte eines verborgenen Meeres
das sammelte in der Muschel deines Ohres die Noten
Brücken–Bausteine
von Hier nach Dort
diese haargenaue Aufgabe
deren Lösung
den Sterbenden mitgegeben wird.

You

You
in the night
busy unlearning the world
from far far away
your finger painted the ice grotto
with the singing map of a hidden sea
which assembled its notes in the shell of your ear
bridge-building stones
from Here to There
this precise task
whose completion
is left to the dying.

Mund

Mund
saugend am Tod
und sternige Strahlen
mit den Geheimnissen des Blutes
fahren aus der Ader
daran Welt zur Tränke ging
und blühte

Sterben
bezieht seinen Standpunkt aus Schweigen
und das blicklose Auge
der aussichtslosen Staubverlassenheit
tritt über die Schwelle des Sehens
während das Drama der Zeit
eingesegnet wird
dicht hinter seinem eisigen Schweisstuch.

Mouth

Mouth
suckling on death
and starry rays
with the blood's secrets
leap out of the vein
on which the world stilled its thirst
and flowered

Dying
occupies its standpoint of silence
and the unseeing eye
of the prospectless dust-forsakenness
transgresses the threshold of seeing
while the drama of time
is consecrated
close behind its icy veronica.

Vergebens

Vergebens
verbrennen die Briefe
in der Nacht der Nächte
auf dem Scheiterhaufen der Flucht
denn die Liebe windet sich aus ihrem Dornenstrauch
gestäupt im Martyrium
und beginnt schon mit Flammenzungen
ihren unsichtbaren Himmel zu küssen
wenn Nachtwache Finsternisse an die Wand wirft
und die Luft
zitternd vor Ahnungen
mit der Schlinge des anwehenden Verfolgers
betet:

Warte
bis die Buchstaben heimgekehrt sind
aus der lodernden Wüste
und gegessen von heiligen Mündern
Warte
bis die Geistergeologie der Liebe
aufgerissen
und ihre Zeitalter durchglüht
und leuchtend von seligen Fingerzeigen
wieder ihr Schöpfungswort fand:
da auf dem Papier
das sterbend singt:

Vainly

Vainly
the epistles burn
in the night of nights
on the pyre of flight
for love winds itself out of its thornbush
flogged in martyrdom
and with its tongue of flames
is beginning to kiss the invisible sky
when vigil casts darknesses on the wall
and the air
trembling with premonition
prays with the noose of the hunter
blowing in with the wind:

Wait
till the letters have come home
from the blazing desert
and been eaten by sacred mouths
Wait
till the ghostly geology of love
is torn open
and its millennia
aglow and shining with blessed pointing of fingers
have rediscovered love's word of creation:
there on the paper
that dying sings:

Es war
am Anfang
Es war
Geliebter
Es war—

It was
at the beginning
It was
My beloved
It was—

Der Schwan

Nichts
über den Wassern
und schon hängt am Augenschlag
schwanenhafte Geometrie
wasserbewurzelt
aufrankend
und wieder geneigt
Staubschluckend
und mit der Luft massnehmend
am Weltall—

The swan

Nothing
above the waters
and at once on the flick of an eye
is suspended
swanlike geometry
rooted in water
vining up
and bowed again
Swallowing dust
and measuring the universe
with air—

In diesem Amethyst

In diesem Amethyst
sind die Zeitalter der Nacht gelagert
und eine frühe Lichtintelligenz
zündete die Schwermut an
die war noch flüssig
und weinte

Immer noch glänzt dein Sterben
hartes Veilchen

The ages of night

The ages of night
are embedded in this amethyst
and an earlier intelligence of light
ignites the melancholy
which then still flowed
and wept

Your dying still shines
hard violet

Death Still Celebrates Life

Der versteinerte Engel

Der versteinerte Engel
noch von Erinnerung träufend
von einem früheren Weltall
ohne Zeit
in der Frauenstation wandernd
im Bernsteinlicht
eingeschlossen mit dem Besuch einer Stimme
vorweltlich ohne Apfelbiss
singend im Morgenrot
vor Wahrheit–

Und die anderen kämmen die Haare vor Unglück
und weinen
wenn die Raben draussen
ihre Schwärze entfalten zur Mitternacht.

The petrified angel

The petrified angel
still dripping memories
of an earlier cosmos
without time
wandering around the women's ward
in the amber light
locked in with the visit of a voice
preworldly, Eden-like
singing in the morning red
with truth—

And the others comb their hair with misfortune
and weep
when the ravens outside
unfold their black wings at midnight.

Wunder der Begegnungen

Wunder der Begegnungen
zweier Geister in der Unterhaltung
über die Leiber hinweg
die trauern wie Waisen
bis in die Zehenspitzen hinein
vor Verlassenheit.

Waschen und Kleiden
sind Gebetanfänge des grossen Sterberituals
im zugigen Durchgang der Ahnungen
die Nacht mit dem Fallobst der Träume
und dem Speicher des Vergessens noch blitzen lässt
aus dem gelobten Lande der äussersten Vision.

Aber wenn auch Heimweh auszog
und der Leib auf dem Laken liegt
—zusammengerollte Fahne der die Freiheit entstieg—
so ist noch nicht der Grad der Finsternis
erreicht wo die Dimension der Auferstehungen beginnt
und die Musik der Sterne abgebrochen wird
von einem Schweigen
das sich im Leben einmal Tod genannt.

Marvel of encounters

Marvel of encounters
of two minds in conversation
far beyond their bodies
that mourn like orphans
down to the tips of their toes
with abandonment.

Washing and dressing
are prayer beginnings of the great death ritual
in the windy passage of premonitions
that night with its windfall of dreams
and storeroom of oblivion still lets flash
from the promised land of the ultimate vision.

But even if longing for home has left
and the body lies on the sheet
—furled flag from which freedom moved out—
even then that degree of darkness
has not been reached where the dimension of resurrections
        begins
and the music of the stars is discontinued
by a silence
that in life once called itself death.

Hinter der Tür

Hinter der Tür
eine Oper wird in die Luft gemimt
die dunkel Besessenen
legen den Äquator des Leidens—ihre flammende Nacht—
um den Leib
während der Liebestrank des Schlafes
auf der Zunge zergeht
und die Arien der Vergangenheit
wie schwarz versickerndes Blut
im Atemzug verröcheln—

O Victoria—schmetternd wie Hähnekrähen—
hinter einer Stirn ist
eine Messerspitze Morgenlicht
in Verzückung geraten—

Behind the door

Behind the door
an opera is mimed into the air
the darkly possessed
place the equator of anguish—their flaming night—
around their bodies
while the love potion of sleep
dissolves on their tongue
and the arias of the past
expire like black oozing blood
in their breath—

O hosanna—resounding like cockcrows—
behind a brow
a knife point of morning light
has become ecstatic—

Noch feiert der Tod

Noch feiert der Tod
das Leben in dir
Närrin in der Spirale der Eile
jeder Schritt weiter entfernt von den kindlichen Uhren
und näher und näher gefasst vom Wind
dem Räuber der Sehnsucht—
Vor Ehrfurcht erheben sich Stühle und Betten
denn die Unruhe ist meerhaft geworden

und Türen—
der Schlüssel auf Abwehr gestellt
ändert die Richtung mit Einlass nach draussen—

Die weissen Schwestern sterngebadet
vom Berühren der Zeichen aus Fremde
von ihm der die Adern hier speist
aus seiner unterirdischen Quelle des Durstes
daran die Visionen sich satt trinken müssen—

Death still celebrates

Death still celebrates
the life in you
fool in the spiral of haste
each step one farther away from the childhood clocks
and ever more closely seized by the wind
the thief of longing–
Chair and bed rise with awe
disquiet has become oceanic

and doors–
the key turned to defense
changes direction with entrance to outside–

The white sisters, bathed in stars,
with touching the tokens of strangeness
his who feeds the veins here
from his subterranean source of thirst
at which the visions have to still themselves–

Aber unter dem Blätterdach

Aber unter dem Blätterdach
vollkommener Vereinsamung
die nur für sich alleine stirbt
wo jeder fremde Blick verscheidet
abstreifend alle Begegnungen
auch die der Liebe

bist du
mit vier Windgesichtern in die Fremde schauend
König über die Gefilde der Unberührbarkeit
eindeutig wie das Gebiss der Toten
das übrig blieb im Staubzerfall
und nur zum Kauen war gesetzt
in seinem Reich
das unterging—

But under the leafy roof

But under the leafy roof
of complete isolation
which dies only its own death
where every strange look dies
casting off all encounters
and love's too

you are
gazing into strangeness with the wind's four faces
king of intangible domains
unmistakable as the teeth of the dead
which survived when all else turned to dust
and were only meant for chewing
in the realm
that perished—

Und die blindgewordenen Leiber

Und die blindgewordenen Leiber
der Ausgestossenen werden
stufenweis
von der Nacht an der Hand genommen
Nacht die ihr eigenes Dunkel überspringt
bis die
geschwisterlich Geführten
zunehmend an Gefährdung
in die Katakomben von Ur hinunterfallen
die begrabenen Schätze betastend
die glimmen im schwarzen Feuer der Leuchter
das wechselt mit weissem Wahrsagelicht
und wieder mit Rot dem Amen der Farben—

Aber die Heilung geschieht auf
neuem Weg
denn niemals kann Eingang
dasselbe wie Ausgang sein
wo Abschied und Wiederkunft
geschieden sind
durch die unheilbare Wunde des Lebens—

Und die Aura der Morgenfrühe
ist schon Antwort und Geschenk
einer anderen Nacht—

And night step by step

And night step by step
takes the blind bodies
of the banished by the hand
Night that leaps over its own darkness
until
led like brother and sister
through increasing danger
they fall into the catacombs of Ur
fingering the buried treasures
which glimmer in the black fire of the candelabra
that alternates with the white light of prophecy
and with red, the amen of color—

But healing occurs
on a new path
for entrance can never be
the same as exit
where farewell and return
are parted by the incurable wound of life—

And the aura of dawn
is answer and gift
of another night—

Zeit der Verpuppung

Zeit der Verpuppung
Zeit der Vergebung
Verfallene mit dem Gesicht im Staub
verspüren schon den Schulternschmerz der Flügel
Wettlauf der Meridiane auf der Sternenhaut
Aderlass der Sehnsucht ins Meer der Verklärung
Herzklopfen der Gestirne
an die Türen der Liebenden
die mit dem Rosenkranz ihrer Münder fortbeten
ihre Leiber in die unsichtbaren Landungen
der Seligkeiten—

Time of pupation

Time of pupation
time of remission
ruined ones with their face in the dust
already sense the shoulder ache of wings
meridians race on the stars' integument
bloodletting of longing into the ocean of transfiguration
heartbeat of constellations
at the doors of lovers
who with their rosary mouths continue to pray
their bodies away into the invisible landings
of the beatitudes—

Die beiden Alten

Die beiden Alten
Hand in Hand sitzend
Zwillingsgestirn
leuchtend noch aus der verbrannten Musik
ihrer Vergangenheit
da sie starben als sie liebten—
verhext von der Magie eines schwarzen Prinzen
dieser ausgeschnittenen Silhouette der Nacht
auf der Netzhaut trauernd wie Schlaflosigkeit
während ihre Zukunft in Nägeln und Haaren
den Tod überwächst—

The old couple

The old couple
sitting hand in hand
twin constellation
still glowing with the burnt music
of their past
when they died as they loved—
bewitched by the magic of a black prince
this excised silhouette of night
like insomnia mourning on the retina
while their future in cuticles and hair
outgrows their death—

Wer ruft?

Wer ruft?
Die eigene Stimme!
Wer antwortet?
Tod!
Geht die Freundschaft unter
im Heerlager des Schlafes?
Ja!
Warum kräht kein Hahn?
Er wartet bis der Rosmarinkuss
auf dem Wasser schwimmt!

Was ist das?

Der Augenblick Verlassenheit
aus dem die Zeit fortfiel
getötet von Ewigkeit!

Was ist das?

Schlaf und Sterben sind eigenschaftslos

Who calls?

Who calls?
My own voice!
Who answers?
Death!
Does friendship end
in the armed camp of sleep?
Yes!
Why does no cock crow?
It waits for the kiss of rosemary
to touch the water!

What is that?

The moment of loneliness
from which time fell
killed by eternity!

What is that?

Sleep and dying are neutral

Die Urkunde vor mir aufgeschlagen

Die Urkunde vor mir aufgeschlagen
in den Stufen der Marmortreppe
die Buchstaben entworfen
in den Kiemen der zeitalternden Wasserwunder

Atem der war
versteinert
und nun wie auf Blitzen mit Füssen
niedergetreten
von uns Beladenen
die wir unwissend verschulden
vieler Minuten Tod—

Und dann
in der Bibel aufgebrochen
weissagend vom wandernden Geheimnis der Seele
und immer zeigend wie mit Fingern aus Gräbern
in die nächste Morgendämmerung—

The archive unfolded before me

The archive unfolded before me
in the steps of the marble stairs
the alphabet outlined
in the gills of age-old water marvels

Breath that was
petrified
and now as on lightning with feet
trampled down by us
who are burdened
and unknowingly cause
many minutes' death—

And then
disclosed in the Bible
prophesying the soul's wandering secret
and always pointing as with fingers from graves
into the next dawn—

Und wundertätig

Und wundertätig
ist der Geist der Luft
zieht auf den Embryo des Weltalls der
wandert frei in unserem Adernetz

Und in der Eichel übernächtig schon
das Schattenreich des Baumes sinnt
und auch Gesang
des Windes Eigentum das er verzehrt

Längst ist das Fliegen schon
dem innern Leib vertraut
er kennt die Sternenstrassen
wie den Staub zuhaus

Aus dem verworfenen Eckstein rinnt die Zeit
die sich am Herzen misst
Das aber schlägt die Ferne furchtbar näher—

And miraculous

And miraculous
is the spirit of air
raises the embryo of the cosmos that
wanders freely in our mesh of veins

And in the acorn, already fatigued,
tree's shadow realm muses
and there is also singing
wind's property which it devours

Long has flying been
an intimate of the inner body
which knows the star streets
like the dust at home

Out of the cast-off cornerstone trickles the time
that takes its measure at the heart
But *that* beats the distance dreadfully nearer—

Schon will äusserstes auswandern

Schon will äusserstes auswandern
das Herz des Wassers
und des Feuers dämonisch verwundertes Licht
die blühenden Geburten der Erde
und Luft die singend den Atem verlässt

Sehnsucht ist der Herrscher
der unsichtbare Adler
zerreisst seine Beute
trägt sie nach Haus—

Extremity is seeking its self-exile

Extremity is seeking its self-exile
the heart of water
and the demonic astonished light of fire
the flowering births of earth
and air which in a song escapes the breath

Longing is the ruler
the invisible eagle
tears its prey apart
and bears it home—

Aber die Sonnenblume

Aber die Sonnenblume
entzündend die Wände
hebt vom Boden
die mit der Seele reden
im Dunkeln

schon Fackeln für eine andere Welt
mit Haaren wachsend bis über den Tod–

Und draussen Finkenschlag
und die Zeit in der Glorie gehend
farbig
und die Blume wachsend
dem Menschen ans Herz

Böses reift in die Kelter
schwarze Traube–verrufene–
schon gepresst zum Wein–

But the sunflower

But the sunflower
that ignites the walls
from the floor raises
those speaking with the soul
in the dark

already torches for another world
with hair growing even beyond death—

And outside: finches singing
and time walking in glory
colorful
and the flower growing
to man's heart

Evil ripens into the casks
black grape—infamous—
already pressed into wine—

Ich kenne nicht den Raum

Ich kenne nicht den Raum
wo die ausgewanderte Liebe
ihren Sieg niederlegt
und das Wachstum in die Wirklichkeit
der Visionen beginnt
noch wo das Lächeln des Kindes bewahrt ist
das wie zum Spiel in die spielenden Flammen geworfen
wurde
aber ich weiss, dass dieses die Nahrung ist
aus der die Erde ihre Sternmusik herzklopfend entzündet—

I do not know the room

I do not know the room
where exiled love
lays down its victory
and the growing into the reality
of visions begins
nor where the smile of the child
who was thrown as in play
into the playing flames is preserved
but I know that this is the food
from which earth with beating heart
ignites the music of her stars—

Die gekrümmte Linie des Leidens

Die gekrümmte Linie des Leidens
nachtastend die göttlich entzündete Geometrie
des Weltalls
immer auf der Leuchtspur zu dir
und verdunkelt wieder in der Fallsucht
dieser Ungeduld ans Ende zu kommen–

Und hier in den vier Wänden nichts
als die malende Hand der Zeit
der Ewigkeit Embryo
mit dem Urlicht über dem Haupte
und das Herz der gefesselte Flüchtling
springend aus seiner Berufung: Wunde zu sein–

The contorted line of suffering

The contorted line of suffering
retracing the supernally ignited geometry
of the cosmos
always on the gleaming tracer path to you
and obscured again in the epilepsy
of this impatience to reach the end—

And in these four walls here nothing
but the painting hand of time
eternity's embryo
with primordial light on the brow
and the heart the shackled fugitive
leaping out of its calling: to be a wound—

Nacht der Nächte

Die Nacht war ein Sarg aus schwarzem Feuer
Die roten Amenfarben der Gebete
bestatteten sich darin

In diesem Purpur wurzelten Zähne—Haare—und der Leib
ein geschüttelter Baum im Geisterwind
Hellgesichtig—dieser Eintags-Cherub
zündete sich an
Die Flammen im Adernetz
liefen alle ihrer Deutung zu

In der Auferstehungsasche spielte Musik

Night of nights

The night was a coffin of black fire
the red amen-colors of prayers
interred themselves inside it

In this purple were rooted teeth—hair—and the body
a shaken tree in the ghostly wind
Lightfaced—this one-day cherub
ignited itself
The flames in the mesh of veins
all rushed toward their significance

Music played in the resurrection ashes

Diese Kette von Rätseln

Diese Kette von Rätseln
um den Hals der Nacht gelegt
Königswort weit fort geschrieben
unlesbar
vielleicht in Kometenfahrt
wenn die aufgerissene Wunde des Himmels
schmerzt

da
in dem Bettler der Raum hat
und auf Knieen gehend
ausgemessen hat alle Landstrassen
mit seinem Leib

denn es muss ausgelitten werden
das Lesbare
und Sterben gelernt
im Geduldigsein—

This chain of enigmas

This chain of enigmas
hung on the neck of night
a king's word written far away
illegible
perhaps in comet journeys
when the torn-open wound of the sky
hurts

there
within the beggar who has room
and crawling upon his knees
has measured out the roads
with his body

for the legible
must be suffered to its end
and dying learned
in patience—

So steigt der Berg

So steigt der Berg
in mein Fenster hinein.
Unmenschlich ist die Liebe,
versetzt mein Herz
in den Glanz deines Staubes.
Schwermut-Granit wird mein Blut.
Unmenschlich ist die Liebe.

Nacht und Tod bauen ihr Land
einwärts und auswärts—
nicht für die Sonne.
Stern ist ein versiegeltes Abendwort—
durchrissen
von der unmenschlichen Auffahrt
der Liebe.

Thus the mountain climbs

Thus the mountain climbs
into my window.
Love is inhuman,
transports my heart
into the splendor of your dust.
My blood becomes a melancholy granite.
Love is inhuman.

Night and death build their land
inwards and outwards—
not for the sun.
Star is a sealed evening word—
ripped
by the inhuman upsurge
of love.

Glowing Enigmas I, II & III

Translated by Michael Hamburger

I

Diese Nacht
ging ich eine dunkle Nebenstrasse
um die Ecke
Da legte sich mein Schatten
in meinen Arm
Dieses ermüdete Kleidungsstück
wollte getragen werden
und die Farbe Nichts sprach mich an:
Du bist jenseits!

Auf und ab gehe ich
in der Stubenwärme
Die Irren im Korridor kreischen
mit den schwarzen Vögeln draussen
um die Zukunft
Unsere Wunden sprengen die böse Zeit
aber die Uhren gehen langsam—

I

This night
I turned the corner into
a dark side street
Then my shadow
lay down in my arm
This tired piece of clothing
wanted to be carried
and the color Nothing addressed me:
You are beyond!

Up and down I walk
in the room's warmth
The mad people in the corridor screech
together with the black birds outside
about the future
Our wounds blast this evil time
but slowly the clocks tick—

Nichtstun
merkbar Verwelken
Meine Hände gehören einem fortgeraubten Flügelschlag
Ich nähe mit ihnen an einem Loch
aber sie seufzen an diesem offenen Abgrund—

Ich wasche meine Wäsche
Viel Sterben im Hemd singt
da und dort Kontrapunkt Tod
Die Verfolger haben ihn mit der Hypnose
eingefädelt
und der Stoff nimmt willig auf im Schlaf—

Lichterhelle kehrt ein in den dunklen Vers
weht mit der Fahne Verstehn
Ich soll im Grauen suchen gehn
Finden ist woanders—

Hinter der Tür
ziehst du an dem Sehnsuchtsseil
bis Tränen kommen
In dieser Quelle spiegelst du dich—

Doing nothing
perceptible wilting
My hands belong to a wingbeat stolen and carried off
With them I am sewing around a hole
but they sigh before this open abyss—

I wash my clothes
Much dying sings in the shift
here and there the counterpoint death
The pursuers have threaded in
together with the hypnosis
and the material absorbs it willingly in sleep—

Effulgence of lights enters into the dark verse
blows with the banner called understanding
I am to go out and search horror
Finding is elsewhere—

Behind the door
you pull on the rope of longing
till tears come
In this wellspring you're mirrored—

Wir winden hier einen Kranz
Manche haben Donnerveilchen
ich nur einen Grashalm
voll der schweigenden Sprache
die hier die Luft blitzen lässt—

Nur Sterben lockt ihnen des Jammers Wahrheit heraus
diese Kehrreime aus Nachtschwärze geschnitten
diese Zungenübungen
am Ende der Tonorgel—

Diese Telegrafie misst mit der Mathematik à la satane
die empfindlich musizierenden Stellen
an meinem Leib aus
Ein Engel aus den Wünschen der Liebe erbaut
stirbt und aufersteht in den Buchstaben
in denen ich reise—

Rufst du nun den einen Namen verzweifelt
aus dem Dunkel—

Here we wind a wreath
Some have violets of thunder
I have only a blade of grass
full of the silent language
that makes this air flash—

Only death draws out of them the truth of misery
these recurring rhymes cut out of night's blackness
these tongue exercises
at the end of the organ of sounds—

This telegraphy measures with the mathematics à la satane
the sensitively music-making places
in my body
An angel builds from the desires of love
dies and rises again in the letters
in which I travel—

If now you desperately call the one name
out of the darkness—

Warte einen Augenblick noch—
und du wandelst auf dem Meer
Das Element durchdringt schon deine Poren
du wirst mit ihm gesenkt und gehoben
und bald im Sand wiedergefunden
und bei den Sternen anfliegender erwarteter Gast
und im Feuer des Wiedersehens verzehrt
still—still—

Ausgeweidet die Zeit
auf deines Angesichtes Bernstein
Das Nachtgewitter zieht flammend heran
aber der Regenbogen
spannt schon seine Farben ein
in den hintergründigen Streifen aus Trost—

Die Fortlebenden haben die Zeit angefasst
bis ihnen Goldstaub in den Händen blieb
Sie singen Sonne—Sonne—
Mitternacht das schwarze Auge
ist mit dem Totenlaken zugedeckt—

Wait a moment longer—
and you walk upon the sea
Already the element transfuses your pores
you are lowered with it and lifted
and found again soon in the sand
and on the stars an awaited guest arriving by air
and consumed in the fire of reunion
                                        be still—be still—

Time's pasture cropped
on the amber of your face
The night thunderstorm approaches flaming
but the rainbow
already is stretching its colors
on to the convex surface of comfort—

Those who live on have clutched at time
until gold dust was left on their hands
They sing sun—sun—
midnight the dark eye
has been covered with the shroud—

Einsamkeit lautlos samtener Acker
aus Stiefmutterveilchen
verlassen von rot und blau
violett die gehende Farbe
dein Weinen erschafft sie
aus dem zarten Erschrecken deiner Augen—

Dein Name ist dir verlorengegangen
aber die Welt eilt herzu
und bietet dir schöne Auswahl an
Du schüttelst den Kopf
aber dein Geliebter
hat dir einmal die Nadel im Heuhaufen gefunden
Hörst du: er ruft dich schon—

Die Betten werden für die Schmerzen zurechtgemacht
Das Leinen ist ihre Vertraute
Sie kämpfen mit dem Erzengel
der niemals seine Unsichtbarkeit verlässt
Steinbeladener Atem sucht neue Wege ins Freie
aber der gekreuzigte Stern
fällt immer wieder wie Fallfrucht
auf ihr Schweisstuch—

Solitude of silent velvety fields
of violas
abandoned by red and blue
violet the going color
your weeping creates it
from the delicate fear of your eyes—

You have misplaced your name
but the world comes running
to offer you a good selection
You shake your head
but your lover
once found your needle for you in a haystack
Listen—he's calling already—

The beds are being made for pain
The linen is pain's close friend
It wrestles with the archangel
who never discards his invisibility
Breath weighed down with stones looks for new ways out
but the crucified star
falls again and again like windfalls
on to pain's shawl—

Wenn ich die Stube beschützt mit Krankheit
verlassen werde—frei zum Leben—zum Sterben—
Luft mit dem Willkommenkuss
den Zwillingsmund tief beglückt
so weiss ich ja nicht
was mein Unsichtbares
nun mit mir anfangen wird—

Ihr sprecht mit mir in der Nacht
aber abgekämpft wie alle Toten
habt ihr den letzten Buchstaben
und die Musik der Kehlen
der Erde hinterlassen
die Abschied durch alle Tonleitern singt
Aber im Flugsand eingebettet
höre ich Neues in der Gnade—

Fürstinnen der Trauer
wer fischt eure Traurigkeiten auf?
Wo finden die Beisetzungen statt?
Welche Meerenge beweint euch
mit der Umarmung eines inneren Vaterlandes?

When I come to leave the room protected by illness
free to live—to die—
air with its welcoming kiss
deeply delights the twin mouth
then I shall not know
what my invisible
will do with me now—

You speak with me in the night
but fought off like all the dead
you have left the last letter
and the music of throats
to earth
that sings farewell up and down all the scales
But bedded in the blown sand
I hear new sounds in grace—

Princesses of sadness
who fishes out your sorrows?
Where do the funerals take place?
What ocean straits weep for you
with the embrace of an inner homeland?

Die Nacht eure Schwester
nimmt Abschied von euch
als letzte Liebende—

Verzeiht ihr meine Schwestern
ich habe euer Schweigen in mein Herz genommen
Dort wohnt es und leidet die Perlen eures Leides
klopft Herzweh
so laut so zerreissend schrill
Es reitet eine Löwin auf den Wogen Oceanas
eine Löwin der Schmerzen
die ihre Tränen längst dem Meer gab—

Schnell ist der Tod aus dem Blick geschafft
Die Elemente machen Aufruhr
doch die knospenden Sphären
drängen schon mit Auferstehung ein
und das Wortlose heilt den erkrankten Stern—

Weine aus die entfesselte Schwere der Angst
Zwei Schmetterlinge halten das Gewicht der Welten für dich
und ich lege deine Träne in dieses Wort:
Deine Angst ist ins Leuchten geraten—

Night your sister
takes leave of you
as the last lover—

Forgive me my sisters
I have taken your silence into my heart
There it lives and suffers the pearls of your suffering
heartache knocks
so loud so piercingly shrill
A lioness rides on the waves of Oceana
a lioness of pains
that long ago gave her tears to the sea—

Quickly death is removed from sight
The elements riot
but the budding spheres
already press in with resurrection
and that which is wordless heals the ailing star—

Weep away the unleashed heaviness of fear
Two butterflies support the weight of the world for you
and I lay your tears into these words:
Your fear has begun to shine—

Im Augenblick schliesst ein Stern sein Auge
Die Kröte verliert ihren mondenen Stein
Du in deinem Bett schenkst der Nacht deinen Atem
O Karte des Universums
deine Zeichen führen das Geäder der Fremdheit
uns aus dem Sinn–

Enterbte beweinen wir Staub–

Meine Liebe floss in dein Martyrium
durchbrach den Tod
Wir leben in der Auferstehung–

Im verhexten Wald
mit der abgeschälten Rinde des Daseins
wo Fussspuren bluten
glühende Rätsel äugen sich an
fangen Mitteilungen auf
aus Grabkammern–

Hinter ihnen
das zweite Gesicht erscheint
Der Geheimbund ist geschlossen–

In one moment a star closes its eye
The toad loses its moonstone
You in your bed give your breath to night
O map of the universe
Your signs show the veins of strangeness
out of our minds—

Disinherited we weep for dust—

My love flowed out into your martyrdom
broke through death
We live in resurrection—

In the bewitched wood
with the pealed-off bark of existence
where footprints bleed
glowing enigmas gaze at each other
intercept messages
from grave vaults—

Behind them
appears the second vision
the secret pact has been made—

Kranke sind dabei aus ihrem Blut
ausgebrochenes Wild wieder einzufangen—
Mit ihren Augen auf Jagd wandernd
dorthin wo der Tag
in todaufgeschreckter Farbe liegt
und die Tiefe des Mondes
in ihren weitoffenen Winterschlaf eindringt
sie hart hochziehend
bis der Faden der Erde reisst
und sie an dem Schneeapfel hängen
mit schlagenden Gliedern—

Meine geliebten Toten
ein Haar aus Dunkelheit
heisst schon Ferne
wächst leise durch offene Zeit
Ich sterbe geheimes Mass füllend
in die Minute
die sich knospend reckt
aber hinterrücks haben sie die Feuerzungen
der Erde aufgepflanzt—
Eine Rebe die ihren Wein der Flamme übergibt
sinke ich rückwärts—

Sick people are about to recapture
wild beasts that broke out of their blood—
Going out to hunt with their eyes
to that place where day
lies in colors startled by death
and the depth of the moon
enters their wide-open hibernation
sharply drawing them upward
until the thread of earth breaks
and they hang on the snow apple
their limbs beating—

My beloved dead
a hair made of darkness even
is called remoteness
softly grows through open time
I die filling a secret measure
into the minute
that budding stretches
but behind my back they have planted
the tongues of fire on to the earth—
A vine that yields its juice to the flame
I sink back—

Während ich hier warte
sehnt sich die Zeit draussen im Meer
aber wird immer wieder an ihrem Blauhaar zurückgezogen
erreicht nicht Ewigkeit—
Noch keine Liebe zwischen den Planeten
aber geheime Übereinkunft zittert schon—

Abendweites Verbluten
bis die Dunkelheit das Grab gräbt
Embryo des Traumes im Mutterleib
klopft an
Die schöpferische Luft bezieht sich langsam
mit der Haut der Neugeburt
Der Schmerz schreibt sich ein
mit dem Fächer der Gesichte
Leben und Sterben geht weiter—

Immer wieder neue Sintflut
mit den herausgefolterten Buchstaben
die an der Angel redenden Fische
im Skelett des Salzes
die Wunde lesbar zu machen—

As I wait here
time yearns out at sea
but is pulled back again and again by its blue hair
does not reach eternity—
Still no love between the planets
but a secret understanding already quivers—

A bleeding away wide as the evening
till darkness digs the grave
embryo of the dream in the womb
knocks
Creative air slowly covers itself
with the skin of new birth
Pain inscribes itself
with the fan of visions
life and death go on—

New Flood again and again
with those letters brought out by torture
those fishes that speak on the hook
in the skeleton of salt
to make legible the wound—

Immer wieder Sterben zu lernen
am alten Leben
Flucht durch die Lufttür
neue Sünde zu holen aus schlafenden Planeten
Äusserste Übung am alten Element des Atems
mit neuem Tod erschreckt
Wo ist die Träne hin
wenn die Erde schwand?

Sie reden Schnee—
Das Stundentuch mit allen vier Weltzipfeln
trägt sich herein
Krieg und Sternenflug hocken beieinander
suchen Schutz dort wo die Nacht
voll Muttermilch überquillt
und mit schwarzem Finger winkt
wo die Neuentdeckungen für die Seelenfahrer harren
funkelnd in Finsternis
tief unter dem Schnee—

To learn dying again and again
from the old life
flight through the door of air
to fetch new sin from sleeping planets
Extreme exercise upon the old element of breathing
startled by new death
What became of the tear
when earth vanished?

They speak snow—
The cloth of hours with its four cosmic ends
bears itself in
war and flight to the stars crouch next to each other
look for asylum where night
overflows with mother's milk
and beckons with a black finger
where new discoveries await the soul explorers
sparkling in darkness
deep underneath the snow—

II

Gesichte aus Dämmerung
Verlorenes der Toten
auch wir hinterlassen
unser Einsamstes den Neugeburten—

Einer dreht sich um
und sieht in die Wüste—
die Halluzination öffnet
die Wand der Sonnenwildnis
wo ein Ahnenpaar
die Sprache des enthüllten Staubes spricht
muschelfern unterm Siegel—

Wir frieren
und kämpfen mit dem nächsten Schritt
in Zukünftiges—

Immer ist die leere Zeit
hungrig
auf die Inschrift der Vergänglichkeit—
In der Fahne der Nacht
mit allen Wundern eingerollt
wissen wir nichts
als dass deine Einsamkeit
nicht die meine ist—
Vielleicht dass ein Traum-verwirklichtes Grün

II

Visions all dusk
lost things of the dead
we also leave to the newly born
what in us is most lonely—

Someone turns round
and peers into the desert—
hallucination opens
the wall of sun wilderness
where an ancestral couple
speaks the language of dust unveiled
remote as a conch, and sealed—

we freeze
and grapple with the next pace
into what's to come—

Always empty time
is hungry
for the inscription of transitoriness—
Furled into night's banner
with all the marvels
we know nothing
save that your loneliness
is not mine—
perhaps a dream-attained green

oder
ein Sang
aus der Vorgeburt schimmern kann
und von den Seufzerbrücken unserer Sprache
hören wir das heimliche Rauschen der Tiefe—

Strasse-Wagen-Füsse
wer weiss noch dass er auf einem Stern wandert
auf einem Flammentopf steht
darin es züngelt süchtig zum Durchstoss
die Geologie der Nächte berührt mit seinem Schritt

Wenn der Schlafverführte
aus dem Brunnen des Morgens
sich erhebt
schuldbeladen
weiss er nicht
dass er noch im Nachtkleid der Larve steckt
denn noch hat er nicht seine Vorgeburt erlebt
noch seinem Tod sich hingegeben

Alles ist im Werden
zwinkert der Schmetterling—

or
a song
from prebirth can glisten
and from the bridges of sighs of our speech
we hear the secret roar of the deeps—

Pavement—cars—feet
who now remembers that he roams a star
that he stands on a caldron of flames
with greedy tongues impatient to break through
that his step touches the geology of nights

When the man seduced by sleep
rises
guilt-laden
from the wellshaft of morning
he does not know
that he is wrapped in the nightclothes of the chrysalis
for still he has not experienced his prebirth
nor abandoned himself to his death

All's metamorphosis
flutters the butterfly—

Ahnungen
wandernde Ähren
auf schwarzem Feld—
liege neben mir
ausgewandert—luftig—
leblose Jenseitsentdeckung
Zwei zu Eins
oder Keins—
die Gesetze im Blitz der Stille verbrannt
am Rande hinausgebeugt
über mein aufgebahrtes Dasein—

In der Zwischenzeit
reist die Liebe zuweilen ins Helle
die alle schützende Nacht
in Scherben schlägt

Posaune
des Jüngsten Tages Licht
mit Adlerflügeln schaudert der Leib
zu hoch entführt—

Premonitions
wandering ears of corn
on a black field—
lie beside me
emigrated—airy—
lifeless discovery of a beyond
Two to One
or None—
the laws consumed in the lightning of stillness
at the rim leaning out
over my life laid on its bier—

In the interim
love at times takes trips into brightness
that smashes to smithereens
all protecting night

Trumpet
Light of Judgment Day
the body quivers with eagles' wings
carried off too high—

Alle Länder haben unter meinem Fuss
ihre grossen Schrecken angewurzelt
die hängen schwer-uralte Ziehbrunnen
immer überfüllend den Abend
das tötende Wort—

So kann ich nicht sein
nur im Stürzen—

Schliesse ich die Augen
Sonnen rollen an ihrer Zeit
goldene Heimat verlassend
und doch bewohnend
Mineral weiss den Weg
in die aufgesparte Ewigkeit
befahrbar nicht mehr
nur bewusstlos in Liebe—

Under my foot all the countries
have rooted their great terrors
that hang heavy-ancient wells
always overfilling evening
the killing word—

I cannot be like that
only in falling—

If I close my eyes
suns push their time
leaving golden homes
yet inhabiting them
Mineral knows the way
to saved-up eternity
no longer passable
save unconscious in love—

Im Meer aus Minuten
jede einzelne verlangt Untergang
Rettung-Hilfe haushoch verschlungene Worte
nicht mehr Luft
nur Untergang
raumlos
nur Untergang
Hoffnung wurde kein Schmetterling
Tod erschaffen so mühsam
Was den Gott verhüllt
auflösen in Sand
dieses Erstlingswort
das in die Nacht stürmt
rettungslos

Erde
Träne unter den Gestirnen—
ich sinke in deinen Überfluss—

In the sea of minutes
each one demands destruction
rescue-help high as houses interlaced with words
no longer air
only destruction
spaceless
only destruction
Hope became no butterfly
to create death with so much effort
Dissolve in sand
that which veils the God
this first word
that rushes into night
beyond rescuing

Earth
Tear among the planets—
I go down in your plenty—

So tief bin ich hinabgefahren
über meine Geburt hinaus
bis ich den früheren Tod traf
der mich wieder verstiess
in diese singende Pyramide
um auszumessen das entzündete
Schweigereich
und ich sehne mich weiss nach dir
Tod—sei mir kein Stiefvater mehr—

Als der grosse Schrecken kam
wurde ich stumm—
Fisch mit der Totenseite
nach oben gekehrt
Luftblasen bezahlten den kämpfenden Atem

Alle Worte Flüchtlinge
in ihre unsterblichen Verstecke
wo die Zeugungskraft ihre Sterngeburten
buchstabieren muss
und die Zeit ihr Wissen verliert
in die Rätsel des Lichts—

So deep I traveled down
beyond my birth
till I met early death
that sent me back again
into this singing pyramid
to survey the inflamed
realm of silence
and whitely I crave you
death—be no stepfather to me now—

When the great terror came
I fell dumb—
Fish with its deathly side
turned upward
air bubbles paid for the grappling breath

All words in flight
to their immortal hiding places
where creative power has to spell
its planetary births
and time loses its knowledge
to the enigmas of light—

Grade hinein in das Äusserste
nicht Versteckspielen vor dem Schmerz
ich kann euch nur suchen
wenn ich den Sand in den Mund nehme
um dann die Auferstehung zu schmecken
denn meine Trauer habt ihr verlassen
abgeschieden seid ihr von meiner Liebe
ihr meine Geliebten—

Wo nur finden die Worte
die Erhellten vom Erstlingsmeer
die Augen-Aufschlagenden
die nicht mit Zungen verwundeten
die von den Lichter-Weisen versteckten
für deine entzündete Himmelfahrt
die Worte
die ein zum Schweigen gesteuertes Weltall
mitzieht in deine Frühlinge—

Immer noch um die Stirn geschlungen
den strengen Horizont der Krankheit
mit dem rasenden Aufstand des Kampfes—
die Rettungsleine in den Abgrund geworfen
das Nacht-Ertrinkende zu fassen—

Straight into the uttermost
no hide and seek with pain
I can only look for you
if I fill my mouth with sand
so as to taste resurrection
for you have left my sorrow
from my love you have departed
you my beloved—

Only where find those words
those illumined by the first sea
those opening their eyes
those not wounded by tongues
those hidden by the light-wise
for your inflamed ascension
those words
which a universe piloted into silence
draws along with it into your Springs—

Still wound about the forehead
the strict horizon of illness
with the raving revolt of conflict—
the lifeline cast into the chasm
to hold one drowning in night—

O-A-O-A-
ein wiegendes Meer der Vokale
Worte sind alle abgestürzt—

Schon in dein Jenseits wuchs
die Figur deines Wesens hinaus
lange ersehnt aus den Fernen
dort wo Lächeln und Weinen
Findlinge werden im Unsichtbaren
die Bilder des Sehens höher verschenkt—

Du aber die Tasten niederdrücktest
in ihre Gräber aus Musik
und Tanz die verlorene Sternschnuppe
einen Flügel erfand für dein Leiden

die beiden Linien von Anfang und Ende
singend sich näherten im Raum—

O-A-O-A-
a rocking sea of vowels
all the words have crashed down—

Already your being's paradigm
has grown into your beyond
long yearned for distantly
in that place where smiling and weeping
become foundlings in the invisible
the images of vision given away to what's higher—

But you pressed down the keys
into their graves of music
and dance the lost meteor
invented a wing for your anguish

the two lines of beginning and end
singing drew closer in space—

Dein Jahrhundert
eine Trauerweide
gebeugt über Unverständliches

Steine trugst du
gepflastert hast du
und wieder aufgerissen
Wundentaufe
und wieder trugst du
das war die Weise
die Tod befohlene
Marterweise—

Einen Punkt im Universum
hast du auf die Schulter geladen
darin Menschenrede
den Tag verschläft
und seelenfein
die Sonne ihr Gold verliert
in die Hand hast du den Stein genommen
der den inneren Tanz lebt
und die Nacht zu Staub zerfallen lässt
wo die namenlose Wanderung beginnt—

Jeder Schritt näher zu dir
doch der Morgen ein blühender Aufenthalt—

Your century
a weeping willow
overhung incomprehensible things

Stones you carried
you paved
and broke up again
the font of wounds
and again you carried
that was the way
the death-commanded
martyr's way—

You lifted on to your shoulders
a point in the universe
in which human speech
sleeps the day through
and delicate as a soul
the sun loses its gold
in your hand you took the stone
which lives the interior dance
and makes night crumble to dust
where the nameless journey begins—

Every pace closer to you
but morning a blossoming sojourn—

Die Nacht königlich tödlich eingeweiht
Eilende über schlafenden Sand
schwarzer Meridian der rieselnden Ferne
um die Wahrheit geschlungen—

Hölle ist nackt aus Schmerz—
Suchen
sprachlos
suchen
Überfahrt in die Rabennacht
mit allen Sintfluten
und Eiszeitaltern umgürtet
Luft anmalen
mit dem was wächst hinter der Haut
Steuermann geköpft mit dem Abschiedsmesser
Muschellaut ertrinkt
Su Su Su

Aber zwischen Erde und Himmel
beten immer noch die gleichen Psalmen
drehen sich in den Köchern aus strahlendem Staub—
Und die Taucher mit göttlichen Grüssen
finden kein Waisenreich
in den rosenroten Wäldern der Tiefe—

Night anointed regally deathly
Hurrying over sleeping sand
black meridian of trickling distance
wound about truth—

Hell is naked with pain—
Seeking
speechless
seeking
Crossing into the raven night
girt with all the Floods
and Ice Ages
to paint air
with that which grows behind the skin
Pilot beheaded with the knife of departure
Hum of sea shell drowns
Su Su Su

But between earth and sky
unchanged as ever the psalms pray
turn in their quivers of radiant dust—
And the divers with divine salutations
find no orphaned realm
in the rose-red woods of the deep—

Wann endlich
hinter dem Ohr
in der Sterbeader
legt sich mein blickloses
Universum zur Ruhe—

Der Umlauf des Blutes
weint seinem geistigen Meer
entgegen
da
wo die blaue Flamme
der Agonie
die Nacht durchbricht—

Lilien am Äquator des Leidens
Als du mit deinen Händen
den Segen sprachst
die Fernen sich näherten
die Meeresverwandten
dem Jenseits zuspülten
der Staub gedächtnislos zu rinnen begann—

Als deine Kinnlade sank
mit dem Gewicht der Erde—

When at last
behind the ear
in the death-vein
will my sightless universe
lie down to rest—

The blood's circulation
weeps toward
its spiritual sea
there
where the blue flame
of agony
bursts through night—

Lilies on the equator of anguish
When with your hands
you pronounced the blessing
distances contracted
those akin to the sea
drifted toward the beyond
and dust without memory began to flow—

When your jaw dropped
with the weight of earth—

III

In meiner Kammer
wo mein Bett steht
ein Tisch ein Stuhl
der Küchenherd
kniet das Universum wie überall
um erlöst zu werden
von der Unsichtbarkeit–
Ich mache einen Strich
schreibe das Alphabeth
male den selbstmörderischen Spruch an die Wand
an dem die Neugeburten sofort knospen
schon halte ich die Gestirne an der Wahrheit fest
da beginnt die Erde zu hämmern
die Nacht wird lose
fällt aus
toter Zahn vom Gebiss–

Dies ist ein Ausflug an eine Stelle
wo die Schatten andere Verträge unterschreiben–
Du sitzest mir abgewandt
dein Rücken durchzieht die Nacht
deine Rede mit dem Gegenüber ist lautlos
Prophezeihungen–fahle Blitze
an der Aschenwand

III

In my room
where my bed stands
a table a chair
the kitchen stove
the universe kneels as everywhere
to be redeemed
from invisibility—
I draw a line
write down the alphabet
paint on the wall the suicidal words
that make the newborn burgeon at once
I have just fastened the planets to truth
when the earth begins to hammer
night works loose
drops out
dead tooth from the gum—

This is an excursion to a place
where the shadows sign other contracts—
you sit turned away from me
your back moves through night
your talk with the other side is mute
prophecies—pale lightning
on the wall of ashes

Im Grünen wird viel gestorben
In den Gräbern seid ihr sandige Nähe—

Und du gingst über den Tod
wie der Vogel im Schnee
immer schwarz siegelnd das Ende—
Die Zeit schluckte
was du ihr gabst an Abschied
bis auf das äusserste Verlassen
die Fingerspitzen entlang
Augennacht
Körperlos werden
Die Luft umspülte—eine Ellipse—
die Strasse der Schmerzen—

Dann einsam
mit dem Schauderflügel
wie die Männer im Polareis
wo Eines immer mit ist über der Zahl—
Der Trauermantel Nacht
hat eine Wunde
deckt nicht—

There's much dying out there in the greenness
You are sandy nearness out there in your graves

And you walked over death
like a bird in snow
always blackly sealing the end—
Time gulped down
whatever you gave it of parting
right to the utmost forsaking
along the fingertips
night of eyes
To grow bodiless
The air was washed all round by—
an ellipse—the street of pains—

Then alone
with the shivering wing
like men in polar ice
where always there is a supernumerary One—
the mourning-cloak night
has a wound
won't cover me—

Bin in der Fremde
die ist behütet von der 8
dem heiligen Schleifenengel
Der ist immer unterwegs
durch unser Fleisch
Unruhe stiftend
und den Staub flugreif machend–

Und ich gedenke ihrer
im Delirium des Absturzes
die ihr Kind aus Luft wieder erschuf
»Dein rechtes Bein vogelleicht–
dein linkes Bein vogelleicht–
tjui tjui–
Locken im Südwind
Herzen können wie Wasser zittern in der Hand
wie Wasser zittern
Augenlid offen aus Tiefe–«

Am in strange parts
protected by the 8
the holy looped angel
He is always on his way
through our flesh
creating unrest
and making dust ripe for flying–

And I think of her
in the delirium of falling
whose child re-created her out of air
"your right leg bird-light–
your left leg bird-light–
tooee tooee–
Call in the south wind
Hearts like water can tremble in one's hand
like water tremble
Eyelid held open by depth–"

Ich sah ihn aus dem Haus treten
das Feuer hatte ihn angebrannt
aber nicht verbrannt
Er trug eine Aktentasche aus Schlaf
unter dem Arm
darinnen war es schwer von Buchstaben und Zahlen
eine ganze Mathematik—
In seinem Arm war eingebrannt:
7337 die Leitzahl
Diese Zahlen hatten sich miteinander verschworen
Der Mann war Raumvermesser
Schon hoben sich seine Füsse von der Erde
Einer wartete oben auf ihn
um ein neues Paradies zu erbauen
»Aber warte nur—balde ruhest du auch—«

Gefangen überall
die Strasse die ich gehe
die Fahrzeuge denen ich ausweiche
Das Eingekaufte verstauen
alles hellsichtige Ausflüge in eure Gebiete—
Strauchelt mein Fuss—schmerzt
ein Umweg in eure Wohnungen—

I saw him step from the house
the fire had singed
but not burned him
He carried a briefcase of sleep
under one arm
heavy inside with letters and figures
a whole arithmetic—
Into his arm was branded:
7337 the ruling number
These numbers had conspired among themselves
The man was a surveyor
Already his feet were rising from the earth
One was waiting for him above
to build a new paradise
"Only wait—you too will soon be at rest—"

Captive everywhere
the street that I walk
the vehicles I avoid
Put away the things I have bought
all visionary excursions into your realms—
My foot trips—hurts
a detour into your dwellings—

Deborah wurde von Sternen zerstochen
und sang doch Siegesgesänge
als die Berge zerflossen
und auf weissglänzenden Eseln wie Wahrsager
die Reiterschar dahinzog

Aber Schweigen ist Wohnort der Opfer—

Ein Spiel wie blinde Kuh
auf grünem Wiesenplan
als die Jungfrauen verfolgt
tödlich schreckgejagd
auf Bäume stiegen
die wuchsen in den Himmel
und sie stürzten in die Leere
das Siebengestirn
verloren die Träne
in der Waisenkolonie—

Wer kann sich verstecken
wie der Fluss im Meer
oder biegen die Nacht
die eisern Schlafende
ins weisse Feuer
das »Offen« schreibt
wenn die Erde ein Fussbreit Jammer ist
unter ihrem Schöpfer—

Deborah was stabbed by stars
and yet sang triumphant hymns
when the mountains dissolved
and on white-gleaming donkeys like prophets
the troop of horsemen moved on

But silence is where the victims dwell—

A game like blindman's buff
on the green meadow
when the virgins pursued
hunted by deadly panic
climbed on to trees
that grew into the sky
and they plunged into the void
the sevenfold constellation
lost the tear
in the orphans' colony—

Who can hide
like a river in the sea
or bend night
brazenly sleeping
into the white fire
that writes "Open"
when earth is five inches of misery
beneath her creator—

Nicht HIER noch DORT
aber im Schlaf doppelzüngig
die Natur stottert in ihren Untergang
der Schatten geht nach Haus
Auf den Lebenslinien wandert der Planet
saugt königliche Botschaften ein
wird reicher—

Sie stiessen zusammen auf der Strasse
Zwei Schicksale auf dieser Erde
Zwei Blutkreisläufe in ihrem Adernetz
Zwei Atmende auf ihrem Weg
in diesem Sonnensystem
Über ihre Gesichter zog eine Wolke fort
die Zeit hatte einen Sprung bekommen
Erinnern lugte herein
Ferne und Nähe waren Eines geworden
Von Vergangenheit und Zukunft
funkelten zwei Schicksale
und fielen auseinander—

Not HERE nor THERE
but double-tongued in sleep
Nature stammers out her decline
the shadow goes home
The planet rambles along the lines of life
sucking in regal messages
grows richer—

They collided in the street
Two destinies on this earth
Two circulations of blood in their arteries
Two that breathed on their way
in this solar system
Over their faces a cloud passed
time had cracked
Remembrance peered in
The far and the near had fused
From past and future
two destinies glittered
and fell apart—

Fortgehen ohne Rückschau–
das letzte Zittergras aus dem Auge reissen
Als Tsong Khapa seinen Meister verliess
wandte er sich nicht nach ihm um
Der Abschied wohnte in seinem Schritt
Die Zeit flammte aus seinen Schultern–

Der Verlassene rief:
»Werft seine Hütte in den Abgrund–«
Und die Hütte schwebte über dem Abgrund
von fünffarbigem Licht durchstochen–
Und der ohne Abschied schritt
in den abgezehrten Ort der nur Geist ist
Und sein Haus war kein Haus mehr
Nur Licht–

Schneller Zeit schneller
wenn die zweite Sekunde die erste auf die Knie drückt
die goldene Armee den ganzen Tag ausgerückt
in der Eile
bis abends alle besiegt sind
ein Rosmarin der Himmel
die Nacht den Tod in seine Ursprungsfarbe wäscht
die Elemente heimwehkrank durchbrennen

Leave without looking back—
tear the last quaking-grass from your eyes
When Tsong-kha-pa left his master
he did not turn to look
Departure dwelt in his stride
Time flared up from his shoulders—

The man left behind cried out:
"Throw his hovel into the chasm—"
And the hovel floated above the chasm
shot through with five-hued light—
And he of no parting strode
into the cropped place that is pure spirit
And his house was no longer a house
Only light—

Faster time faster
when the second second forces the first to its knees
the golden army all day long on the march
in haste
till at evening all have been beaten
a rosemary bush the sky
night washes death down to its primal color
the elements sick with nostalgia break loose

zum Meer laufen
atemlos werden
das Blühen verweigern
denn es starb wieder Einer
der die Zeit mass—

Ich schreibe dich—
Zur Welt bist du wieder gekommen
mit geisternder Buchstabenkraft
die hat getastet nach deinem Wesen
Licht scheint
und deine Fingerspitzen glühen in der Nacht
Sternbild bei der Geburt
aus Dunkelheit wie diese Zeilen—

Den Schlaf die Decke der Siebenschläfer
über sich ziehn
Das Verstossene in der Wunde
und Widderblitze vom Jüngsten Gericht
verstecken mit Siegeln—
Aber erst das blutig gegeisselte Wort
bricht in die Auferstehungen ein
die Seele am Flügel—

run to the sea
grow breathless
refuse to blossom
for another has died
who took time's measure—

I write you—
You have come into the world again
with the haunting strength of letters
that groped for your essence
Light shines
and your fingertips glow in the night
Constellation at the birth
of darkness like these verses—

Pull over oneself
sleep the blanket of the seven sleepers
Hide with seals
that in the wound which was exiled
and ram-lightning of the Last Judgment—
But only the word lashed bloody
breaks into resurrection
the soul on its wing—

Dunkles Zischeln des Windes
im Getreide
Das Opfer zum Leiden bereit
Die Wurzeln sind still
aber die Ähren
wissen viele Muttersprachen–

Und das Salz im Meer
weint in der Ferne
Der Stein ist eine feurige Existenz
und die Elemente reissen an ihren Ketten
zur Vereinigung
wenn die Geisterschrift der Wolken
Urbilder heimholt

Geheimnis an der Grenze des Todes
»Lege den Finger an den Mund:
Schweigen Schweigen Schweigen«–

Vier Tage vier Nächte
war ein Sarg dein Versteck
Überleben atmete ein–und aus–
Tod zu verspäten–
Zwischen vier Brettern
lag das Leiden der Welt–

Dark hissing of the wind
in the corn
The victim ready to suffer
The roots are still
but the ears of corn
know many native languages—

And the salt in the sea
weeps afar
The stone is a fiery being
and the elements tug on their chains
to be united
when the ghostly script of the clouds
fetches home primal images

Mystery on the border of death
"Lay a finger upon your lips:
Silence Silence Silence"—

Four days four nights
a coffin was your hiding place
Survival breathed in—breathed out—
to delay death—
Between four boards
lay the world's anguish—

Draussen wuchs die Minute voller Blumen
am Himmel spielten Wolken—

Das Samenkorngeheimnis geworfen
wurzelt schon in der Zukunft
setzt an:
Ein Tanz in den Ardennen
unterirdisches Suchen
nach dem Gesicht im Bergkristall
Morgenröte im Nichts über
dem Südmeer
Liebende
halten die Muschel mit dem Konzert
der Tiefsee ans Ohr
Ein Stern öffnet sich zum Eingang
Der Mond hat Besuch gehabt
Der Greis kehrt nicht wieder
Eine Geburt saugt am Leben—

Outside grew the minute full of flowers
over the sky clouds played—

Thrown the seed grain's mystery
already strikes root in the future
begins:
A dance in the Ardennes
subterranean seeking
for the face in the rock crystal
Dawn in the Nothingness above
the South Sea
Lovers
hold to their ears the conch
with the deep-sea concert
A star opens to an entrance
The moon has had visitors
The old man does not return
A birth sucks at life—

ELI: A Mystery Play of the Sufferings of Israel

Translated by Christopher Holme

Characters

Washerwoman	Man with a Mirror
Baker Woman	The Dajan
Samuel	Beggar
Jossele	Rabbi
Girls	Old Woman
Bricklayers	Old Man
Michael	Carpenter
Peddler Mendel	Gardener
Woman	Creature
Man	Farmer
Knife Grinder	Teacher
Hunchback	Shoemaker
Blind Girl	His Wife
Fiddler	Postman
Young Woman	Doctor
Crowd of Worshippers	Children

Various Voices

Time

After Martyrdom

Scene One

Marketplace of a small Polish town, in which a number of survivors of the Jewish people have come together. The houses around about in ruins. Nothing but a fountain in the middle, at which a man is working, cutting and laying pipes

WASHERWOMAN (*carrying a basket full of white linen. Chanting*)

From the laundry, the laundry I come
from washing the garments of death,
from washing the shirt of Eli,
washing out the blood, washing out the sweat,
child-sweat, washing out death.

(*To the pipelayer*)
To you, Samuel, will I bring it,
to the Cattle Lane bring it at evening,
where the bats flutter around in the air
as I flutter the Bible pages
looking for the Song of Lamentation
where it burns and smokes and the stones fall.
Your grandson's shirt will I bring you,
the shirt of Eli.

BAKER WOMAN

How came it, Biddy, that he was struck dumb?

WASHERWOMAN

It was on the morning when they fetched the son,
tore him from bed, from sleep—

as they had torn open the door
to the Shrine of Shrines in the Temple—
forbid, forbid—
thus they tore him from sleep.
Rachel his wife, too, they tore from sleep,
drove her before them through the Cattle Lane,
the Cattle Lane—the widow Rosa sat
at the corner, at the window
and told the story of how it happened
until they shut her mouth
with a thorn, because her husband was a gardener.
Eli in his nightshirt ran after his parents,
his pipe in his hand,
the pipe he had played in the fields
to lamb and calf—
and Samuel, the grandfather,
ran after his grandson.

And when Eli saw,
saw with the eyes of an eight-year-old
how they drove his parents
through the Cattle Lane, the Cattle Lane,
he put the pipe to his mouth and blew it.
And he did not blow it
as one who pipes to his cattle or in play,
said the widow Rosa while she was yet alive,
no, he threw back his head
like the stag or the roebuck
before it drinks at the spring.
He pointed the pipe to heaven,
he piped to God, did Eli,
said the widow Rosa while she was yet alive.

Baker Woman

Come aside, Biddy, so that he may not hear,
hear our talk, the dumb one.
Must like a sponge else suck in our words,
can bring nothing forth from his throat,
tied tight with death.

(*They go aside*)

Washerwoman

A soldier marching with the procession
looked around and saw Eli
piping to high heaven,
struck him down dead with his rifle butt.
A young soldier he was, very young still,
said the widow Rosa.
Samuel took up the corpse,
sat down upon a milestone,
and is dumb.

Baker Woman

Was not Michael then at hand
to come to the rescue of Eli?

Washerwoman

Michael was in the house of prayer,
in the burning house of prayer,
he checked the flames,
he saved Jossele,
saved Dajan,
saved Jacob,
but Eli is dead.

BAKER WOMAN (*meditating*)

And would perhaps have come to an end with him,
the moment
when HE forsook us?

WASHERWOMAN

And the widow Rosa added too
that Michael came a minute too late,
a tiny minute,
look, tiny as the eye of my needle
with which I had just been sewing up the torn seam
of Eli's shirt.
Why do you think he came too late,
he whom no enemy detained?
He took one step into the side street,
a single step,
there where the house of Miriam once stood,
and then he turned around—
and Eli was dead.
Then said the widow Rosa:
But Michael has the unbroken vision,
not like ours which sees only fragments—
he has the Baalshem vision,
from one end of the world to another—

(*She approaches the fountain*)

Samuel, will it be ready for the Feast,
for New Year, the fountain?

SAMUEL *nods*

BAKER WOMAN

I'll tell you, Biddy, a secret.
I hear the footsteps!

Washerwoman

What footsteps do you hear, Basia?

Baker Woman

When they fetched Isaac, my husband,
the baker, because he baked the pretzels,
the sugar pretzels with forbidden flour,
when they fetched him from the ovens,
I gave him his overcoat,
because the cold outside was cutting—
they whinnied like horses
whinnying with joy at their oats—
"He'll be back, quicker than he can put it on—
he'll be back!"
He came back, without footsteps!
That's when the footsteps began in my ear!
The heavy footsteps,
the strong footsteps,
they said to the earth:
I'll break you open—
in between, his dragging step,
for he walked little,
breathed heavily in the cold,
at the ovens he stood,
by day and by night—

Washerwoman

Do you hear the footsteps still?

Baker Woman

They live in my ear,
they walk in the daytime

they walk in the nighttime,
whether you speak or I speak,
I hear them always.

WASHERWOMAN
Ask Michael
if he can rid you of the footsteps.
I must ask Michael what he knows.
For he stitches sole to uppers,
he must know more than just how to wander to the grave.
Let me tell you, Basia, I'm a washerwoman,
I've made the lye, I've washed, I've rinsed,
but today at the laundry,
there where the seam was torn on Eli's shirt—
there it looked at me—

BAKER WOMAN
If only I could,
I'd open the seam above there,
made bloody by the sun,
could Isaac's eyes but see me—
I'd say,
caught behind bars I am,
bars made of footsteps,
open the bars,
let me out of the heavy footsteps,
the strong footsteps
which break open the earth—
in between, your dragging step—

WASHERWOMAN
The fountain's running!

BAKER WOMAN

The fountain's running!

(She cups her hands and drinks)

Take away the footsteps,
the footsteps from my ear—
the footsteps—footsteps—

(She falls to the ground)

Curtain

SCENE TWO

The same marketplace, seen from a different angle. The fountain plays. At one of the ruined houses an old bricklayer and his apprentice are working. In the background a narrow, ruined alley at the end of which the prayer tent can be seen. Green landscape gleams through everywhere

BRICKLAYER

Jossele, fill the bucket at the fountain,
run for the lime there where they're building,
building outside the gates the new town.
No gates are there any more,
no old town any more.
No house of prayer any more,
only earth enough for the holy ground.

(To himself)
This was a house, here, this was a hearth,
there's a saucepan still, burned black.
Here's a colored ribbon,

perhaps it was a cradle bow—
perhaps it was an apron string—
who knows?
Here's a skullcap.
Who wore it?
A young man or an old one or a boy?
Did it guard the Eighteen Benedictions, the silent ones,
from idle thoughts,
from wicked thoughts,
or—who knows?

A WOMAN *in a nightdress hurries up the narrow alley, knocking with her finger on walls and stones*

BRICKLAYER
Esther Weinberg, what're you knocking at?
There's no answer locked in the stone.

JOSSELE (*with the bucket*)
The woman has run out of the infirmary,
now she's picking up stones and throwing them away—

BRICKLAYER
Wants to break out of her prison—

JOSSELE
But what is she doing now?
Opening and shutting her hands like cups
and filling them with air.

STONEMASON'S WIFE (*singing*)
Your right leg
light as a bird—

your left leg
light as a bird—
curls in the south wind—
hearts can shiver like water in the hand—
shiver like water—
Oh . . . Oh . . .

(*She runs off*)

BRICKLAYER
She makes her child out of air—

(*He takes a stone*)

We make graves,
but she has broken out already—
is taking lessons already with HIM—

JOSSELE (*runs after the woman and returns*)
The woman is dead.
Said to a stone: "Here I come,"
struck her brow upon it and died.
This letter was lying beside her.

BRICKLAYER (*reading*)
"Finely veined like your temples was the stone.
Laid it to my cheek before going off to sleep,
felt its depressions,
felt its elevations,
its smooth and jagged places—
blew upon it,
and it breathes like you, Esther . . ."
This is from Gad, her husband,
who slaved himself to death in the quarry,
bearing Israel's burden—

JOSSELE *weeps and sighs*

BRICKLAYER

Don't cry, Jossele.
Let us build the old house anew.
If tears hang on the stonework,
if sighs hang on the woodwork,
if the little children can't sleep,
death has a soft bed.

(He lays bricks, singing and whistling)

Master of the world!
Thou, Thou, Thou, Thou!
Master of all stones!
Thou, Thou, Thou, Thou!
Where can I find Thee,
and where can I not find Thee?
Thou, Thou, Thou, Thou!

Curtain

SCENE THREE

The ruined alley near the marketplace, which can just be seen. The fountain plays. Children come running

OLDER GIRL

The schoolteacher said
today was the day
of Michael's wedding years ago,
the day they snatched his bride from him
before the blessing of the candles.

Younger Girl
What shall we play?

Older Girl
Wedding and candle-blessing
and I'll be the bride—

Boy (*seizing her*)
And I'll snatch you away.

Older Girl (*freeing herself*)
No, I don't want that,
I'll find myself a baby to cradle.

Jossele
When I went on the ship,
the sea always traveled away with us
like the roll of yarn
when I make it pop up on the thread,
but we didn't reach the white
where it begins.
But in sleep I was there.
When I woke up, someone said:
Many are drowned,
but you are saved.
But often the water still follows me.

Younger Girl
I sat deep below in the night,
and there was a woman there,
as kind as Sister Leah from the infirmary
and she said: Sleep, I'll watch.
And then there came a wall in my mouth
and I ate a wall.

Older Girl

Was the woman your mother?

Younger Girl

Mother? what's that?

Older Girl *(pulling a rag out of the rubble)*

Here is linen,
and here's a piece of wood
charred only at one end.
Now I've got a baby,
a baby with black hair,
And now I'll cradle it.

(Singing)
Once on a time there was a tale—
the tale is not a gay one,
the tale begins with singing
about a king of the Jews.

Once on a time there was a king—
a king there was, he had a queen,
the queen she had a vineyard—
Lyulinka, my child . . .

Younger Girl

Did you learn that from Becky?

Older Girl

Yes.

(Singing)
The vineyard it had a tree,
the tree it had a bough,

the bough it had a little nest—
Lyulinka, my child . . .

JOSSELE
Look, I've found a bone—
who makes himself a pipe of dead men's bones
will never pipe the cattle forth—

OLDER GIRL
Does the water still follow you?

JOSSELE
Yes, sometimes,
but more often it is the hanged Isidor who comes
and says: My friend, a roll of yarn
holds like a rope—

OLDER GIRL
It's late,
let's go to Becky.

JOSSELE
Give me your baby,
I'll throw it on the rubble,
there it can cry.

OLDER GIRL
No, don't do that,
Miriam its name is,
and I'll go into the kitchen,
and ask Becky for a whisk,
that'll do for a head.

(*Singing*)
The nest it had a little bird,
the bird it had a little wing,
the wing it had a little feather—
Lyulinka, my child . . .

(*As they all go off slowly, singing from backstage*)
The king he had to die,
the queen she had to perish,
the tree had to shatter,
the bird fly from its nest . . .

Curtain

SCENE FOUR

MICHAEL'S *cobbler's shop in the only unruined house. Through the window, moonlight and open fields. Shelves on the walls with shoes on them. Table with tools. Bench before the window.* MICHAEL, *tall, thin, with reddish hair. He snatches a pair of shoes and puts them on the window bench. Then he lifts up a shoe, so that it is silhouetted in black against the moonlight. It is a small woman's shoe*

MICHAEL

You trod so lightly,
the grasses rose behind your feet.
Here is the strap you tore,
as you hurried toward me, that time—
quick is love,
the sun as it rises
is slower far.
Miriam—

(*He sinks to the ground, his head between his knees*)

What constellation saw your death?
Was it the moon, the sun, or the night?
with stars, without stars?

A cloud passes across the moon. The room is almost dark. Gliding footsteps are heard. A sigh, then a rough man's voice

MAN'S VOICE

Thou art fair, my love,
were I thy bridegroom
I should be jealous of death,
but thus—

Wild laughter, screams

MICHAEL *lies for a long time motionless. The moon shines again. He raises himself, snatches up a pair of heavy men's shoes*

MICHAEL

Isidor's shoes,
the pawnbroker's shoes,
heavy shoes.
A worm is stuck to the sole,
a trodden worm.
The moon shines on,
just as when it saw your death.

(*He sinks to the ground in the same position as before. Heavy footsteps are heard*)

FIRST VOICE

Don't hang it up,
I've got it in a casket,

of sandalwood the casket is—
was the jewel case of the rich, then poor, Sarah—
good customer she was—

SECOND VOICE

Speak, what about the casket?

FIRST VOICE

Buried it, behind the beech tree,
the only beech tree among the pines—
there's a ring inside,
has a stone, an aquamarine,
has a blue fire, the aquamarine—
the whole Mediterranean is in it—
blue, so blue, when the sun plays—
No—in the pockets nothing rattles, empty—
That's the night wind,
rattling silver in the leaves—

SECOND VOICE

Rattle on then with the night wind, you—

MICHAEL *lies motionless. He gets up again, snatches a pair of child's shoes and lifts them above his head. The morning sun begins to redden the sky*

MICHAEL

Shoes,
trodden over on the inside,
lamb's wool sticking to them—
Eli—

(*He sinks into the same position as before. The rending notes of a pipe are heard*)

Curtain

Scene Five

Room of a ruined building. Samuel *sits on a bed of boards. On his lap is Eli's death shirt. A candle flickers.* Michael *enters*

Michael

Samuel,
I pray you to help me find what I am seeking,
I seek the hand,
I seek the eyes,
I seek the mouth,
I seek the piece of skin,
into which the corruption of this earth has entered,
I seek Eli's murderer.
I seek the dust
which since Cain has mingled
with every murderer's dust and waited,
meanwhile has formed birds perhaps—
and then murderers.
Perhaps it formed the mandrakes
for which Rachel gave up a night to Leah—
Perhaps it encased Sammael's exhalations of hate—
To think
that this dust may have touched the prayer book of Luria,
when it lay hidden,
till its letters spouted flames—
to think—
Oh, what dust is it that I bring you here on my shoes.

(*He takes off his shoes*)

Samuel, let me ask your dumbness,
Was he tall?

SAMUEL *shakes his head*

MICHAEL
Was he shorter than I and taller than you?

SAMUEL *nods*

MICHAEL
His hair, was it fair?

SAMUEL *nods*

MICHAEL
His eyes, black, blue?

SAMUEL *shakes his head*

MICHAEL
Gray?

SAMUEL *nods*

MICHAEL
His color, red-cheeked, healthy?

SAMUEL *shakes his head*

MICHAEL
Pale then?

SAMUEL *nods*

MICHAEL (*sobbing*)

How many millions of men has the earth?
Murderers like Cain.
Crumbled mandrakes,
nightingale dust,
Dust of prayer books,
from which letters spring out like flames.

SAMUEL *hands* MICHAEL *a shepherd's pipe.* MICHAEL *breathes into it. A weak note is heard. He points to the death shirt, on which the form of a man's head is silhouetted*

Look, oh look,
the candle throws the shadow—
or your dumbness speaks:
Very young still,
the nose is broad,
its nostrils quiver with blood lust,
the eyes have the pupils of a wolf—
The mouth is small as a child's—

The face disappears

Thus faces are compounded in dreams—
water poured from the invisible—
It is gone
and burns in my eyes.
Until I find him
it will get between me and everything on this earth,
it will hang in the air—
In the bread I eat

this nightmare dust will be my food.
In the apple I eat
the murderer's face will lurk—
Samuel,
your speech has already reached
where all dust is at an end.
Beyond the Word this thing was compounded.

(*He backs to the door, where he puts on his shoes*)

Curtain

Scene Six

Open side of the marketplace, giving on to the fields. The splashing of the fountain is heard. On a sandy path in plowland, Peddler Mendel *stands and cries his wares, surrounded by onlookers*

Mendel

Bargain offer! Amazing opportunity!
It is my privilege to show you:
Apron material, washable, colorfast, with flower designs,
with butterfly designs,
Stockings of wool, stockings of silk, straight from Paris.
Elastic, look, you can stretch it
from here to kingdom come, and back it springs—
direct from America.
From England I have lavender for headaches
and peppermint for a bad digestion—
But this linen now from Russia—
not now for the dead, no longer,

not for the feet pointing toward the door—
no, for the lovely bride, for baby too—

WOMAN (*to her husband*)
Look here,
what a holiday dress that'd make for me,
just now with the New Year coming in.

MAN
We live in the poorhouse,
you have neither table nor chair,
what do you want with such stuff?

WOMAN
Why, look now,
the little Sterntal woman
has a better husband than I,
he's bought her the fine scarf already.

MAN
Where you now stand, it ran with blood—
We are saved

WOMAN
and ought to have joy in our safety.

MAN (*to the* PEDDLER)
You're spoiling the women all over again.
This love of finery
will bring even mourning crepe out in pleats and flounces.

MENDEL
I have no wife,
but if I had one, I'd vie with Solomon.

He who praises the virtuous wife
praises her attire as well—

MAN

Very well, measure me a length of the stuff.

KNIFE GRINDER

Scissors to grind,
Knives to grind,
Sickles for the new crop—

ANOTHER WOMAN

I wish he'd be off
and do his grinding away from here—
The noise of knives grinding
Is more than a body can stand—

KNIFE GRINDER

Next time you eat
you'll need a knife—
Next time you harvest
you'll need a knife—
When next you dress
two knives you'll need.

(*He grinds on*)

OTHER WOMAN

A lot it matters to you—
or don't you feel it? that your grinding
carves up the world in pieces.

KNIFE GRINDER

I hate nobody,
want to give no offense—
I grind because it's my trade—

OTHER WOMAN

So it's his trade,
as it's mine to weep—
and another's to die.

Two teenage girls go across

ONE GIRL (*speaking to the* PEDDLER)

Peddler, I want to buy a hank of woolen yarn.

(*To her companion*)
Let me lay the hank around your wrists.
You hold them still while I wind
and it's like saying goodbye.
Me they held fast by the wrists
and took my mother away—
and the goodbye went from her to me—
from me to her,
till it was at an end—

They walk on. A FIDDLER *has come and starts to play. They all begin to dance*

HUNCHBACK

What longing in the bones—
the old Adam ferments in the notes,
the new man has his first rib already.

BLIND GIRL *comes with hands stretched before her, holding twigs and sticks. She is barefoot and dressed in rags*

GIRL (*coming to a halt in front of the* FIDDLER)

There's a twitching under my foot.
The pavement of our longing must be here at an end.
There go all my journeys.

(*She throws down the sticks*)

Always, when my feet got a new wound
a journey was at an end
like a clock that strikes.
I wanted to see my love once more
but then they took away my eyes—
from that time on, I counted midnight.
Now I am but a tear removed from my love,
and the last wound has opened in my foot—

(*She sinks to the ground and is taken away*)

HUNCHBACK

She's brought with her only the skeleton of her
   journeys—
The flesh is all consumed with longing—
She wanted to see her love once more—
but the Devil
shies from the mirror of love in a human look
and shattered it—

TWO CHILDREN (*collect the twigs and sing*)

We've got sticks,
we've got journeys,
we've got bones,
ei, ei, ei—

MENDEL

This one stick
I could use to tie up my bundle,
the others you can keep.

FIDDLER *plays on, and everybody dances*

HUNCHBACK

Don't dance so heavily
knocking at the walls of sleep—
it could flood you,
too many young hearts inside them—
there'll be love dust—
Who knows how that grain will taste—
who knows?

YOUNG WOMAN (*with a child on her arm, to the* HUNCHBACK)

Don't stare at my child like that!
God preserve it from the evil eye—

HUNCHBACK

Forbid that I should scorch it with my look.
I only wonder
how you were able to bear it
in these times—

YOUNG WOMAN

In a hole in the earth I bore it,
in a hole I suckled it—
Death took its father,
me he did not take,
saw the milk in my breasts
and did not take me.

HUNCHBACK (*repeating her words*)

And did not take you—

YOUNG WOMAN

Forgive me if I offended you.
But God preserve me,
I thought at first

you were a living piece
of Israel's misfortune.

HUNCHBACK (*pointing to his hump*)
You saw the satchel
in which the scapegoat carries its people's misfortune.

YOUNG WOMAN
To me it seems
a hundred or more years have passed
since I sat in my hole—
I can't bear the light any more—
I only blink—
To me these seem not human beings,
mounds of earth I see dancing—
night can preserve no names.
Whatever barks, whatever sings
I've long forgotten—

HUNCHBACK (*pointing to the long shadows thrown by the* PEDDLER)
It's a late hour already in Israel.

All the dancers throw long shadows. Their bodies are as if blotted out by the glare of the evening sun. Only the YOUNG WOMAN *with her child stands out clearly in the light*

Curtain

SCENE SEVEN

Marketplace as at the beginning. In the background the narrow alley ending in the prayer tent. A CROWD OF WORSHIPPERS *is gathering for the Festival Service*

FIRST WORSHIPPER

Here is the place
where baker Isaac of the shuffling gait
was struck down because of a sugar pretzel.
His shop sign was an iron pretzel,
on it the children's eyes
had fastened with longing,
and eaten their fill of it—
One child fell dead,
had eaten enough.
Thought Isaac,
I'll bake a sugar pretzel,
then another and once again,
so that they'll not eat themselves to death
with their eyes on the iron pretzel.
One pretzel he baked, no more.
The iron pretzel glowed
as in the baker's oven fire,
until a man of war took it away,
melted it down for the next death.

A MAN *with a looking glass in his hand passes by, looking into it*

MAN

There, where you carried your children—
I believe we were seven in number—
there your body collapsed on to the grave gaping below,
your withered breasts hung over it in mourning.
O my mother,
your murderer held a mirror before you
so that you might have a comic death—
Mother, you looked at yourself

until your jaw sagged on to your breast—
but the great Angel spread his wings over you!
Through the barbed wire of the times
he came hasting to you
with torn wings—
for iron and steel have grown rampant, Mother,
building primeval forests in the air—
murderers' brains have grown rampant—
vines of premeditated anguish sprouting from them.
Mirror, mirror,
echo from the forest of the dead—
victims and hangmen,
victims and hangmen
played with their breath upon you the dying game.
Mother,
one day there'll be a constellation called Mirror.

(*He passes on*)

SECOND WORSHIPPER (*to* THIRD WORSHIPPER)
Is he still saying kaddish into the mirror?

THIRD WORSHIPPER
Yes. Holy Baalshem,
last sheaf-carrier of Israel's strength,
weaker your people has become and weaker,
a swimmer
whom only death brings to land.

THE DAJAN
But I tell you:
Many a one of you has had the potent faith,
behind the curtain of night

has forced down
the great tranquilizers life and death.

(Pointing to a house wrecked by gunfire)
Not with such weapons alone was the battle fought,
I tell you:
Battlefields there are—battlefields
which the inventors of daylight murder
have never dreamed of.
Many a prayer
has hung with flaming wings before the cannon's
mouth,
many a prayer
has burned up the night like a sheet of paper!
Sun, moon, and stars have been arrayed by Israel's
prayer
along the potent strings of faith—
diamonds and carbuncles
about the dying throat of her people
O! O!—

HUNCHBACK
They say,
because of my jerking shoulders
they hate me—

KNIFE GRINDER
They say,
because of my perpetual smile
they hate me—

MENDEL
They say,
because of this heap of stone

which was once my house
they hate me—

BEGGAR *with a feather in his hat*

When I turn the hat over
it's a grave for money,
or I put it on,
and it's something
which has to do with flying.
What are riches in a Jew
but an ice pit around a frozen tear!—

THE DAJAN

I see,
see the beginning of your jerking shoulders, Simon—
when with Abraham you dug the well of the "Seven Oaths"
in Beersheba—
I see,
I see the beginning of your smile, Aman—
on Horeb planted in the seventy elders,
to sprout again
sprout in the wandering dust of the lip.
Stones are stones—
Earth of Paradise in them, but in greed destroyed.
But they do not know the beginning,
not the eternal beginning—
and that's why they hate us—

ALL THE BYSTANDERS

That's why they hate us—

THE DAJAN (*shouting*)

Eli, because of you,
to know your beginning—

(*He collapses*)

Curtain

SCENE EIGHT

The same. THE WORSHIPPERS *have disappeared into the prayer tent. Murmurs are heard, then the voice of the* RABBI *pronouncing the Shophar lines*

VOICE OF THE RABBI

Tekiá—

A long note is heard, of a single pitch

VOICE

Shevarim—

Three notes in succession

VOICE

Teruá—

A trilled note

The shadow of the seven-branched candlestick is silhouetted on the tent wall. The tent is opened. The worshippers march out

FIRST WORSHIPPER

The air is new—
gone is the smell of burning,
gone is the smell of blood,
gone is the smell of smoke—
the air is new!

SECOND WORSHIPPER

In my ear there's a noise
as if someone were pulling
the barb from the wound—
the barb that is sticking in the middle of the earth—
Someone takes the two halves of the earth apart
like an apple,
the two halves of today and yesterday—
takes out the maggot
and joins the casing together again.

THE WORSHIPPERS *march across the marketplace*

SEVERAL WORSHIPPERS

Happy New Year!
May the moment when He forsook us
be at an end!

OTHERS JOINING THEM

And Israel emptied forth its soul for death—

OTHERS

The horn has sounded to call us home.
He did not forget us.
On the palms of both hands engraved
has He His people!

Everyone has gone off, the marketplace is empty.
AN OLD WOMAN *comes and sits on the edge of the fountain*

OLD WOMAN

Isn't he coming yet, the Rabbi?
Still not here yet, the Rabbi—

(*She gets up and goes to meet him, weeping*)

There comes the Rabbi!
A cake I baked
in the oven out there in the fields—
the other women said:
That's a fine cake you've baked,
your holiday cake. I said,
It's for the Rabbi, the cake.
I took three measures of flour,
as Sarah did when she baked for the angels,
the angels
when they came to Abraham at evening—

RABBI

There's nothing in the scripture
about their coming at evening—

OLD WOMAN

Always the angels come at evening.
And the water at the spring
has a mouth that speaks.

RABBI

Why are you crying, Grandma?

Old Woman

Have I not a right to cry?
The rats have eaten the cake,
the cake for the Rabbi.

Rabbi

New flour will be given you
and we'll eat the cake together—

Old Woman

Can't bake any more,
can't eat any more,
can only weep.

(*Weeping more violently*)

Rabbi

Do you live in the house with the old people,
Grandma?

Old Woman

I live in the third cellar
on the marketplace.

Rabbi

Why don't you live with the old people?

Old Woman

Because I must live
there where I live.
Yehudi was born there,
Natel was born there,
Taubel was born there—
their cry is still in the place,

and Taubel's dance is in the place—
Michael gave me a pair of shoes
because the grave-earth had entered into the old ones,
Yehudi's earth,
Taubel's earth,
Natel's earth.
They're shoes from Rabbi Sassow,
they're Tsaddick shoes,
holy shoes, holy dancing shoes.

(*She laces them up tighter*)

Taubel's dancing is in them.
Look!

(*She begins to dance*)

Curtain

SCENE NINE

Marketplace at the fountain. THE GIRLS *fill the jugs and hand them to the dusty bricklayers as they pass, building the new town*

BRICKLAYER (*to a girl*)
Thanks for the drink,
I am going now to build the new town.

GIRL
Cement this in too.
It's got the Holy Words in it,
given to me by my love,
and I wore them on this chain about my neck.

BRICKLAYER

How can one part with such a gift?

GIRL

Short my life will be,
but the walls,
they must hold.

SECOND BRICKLAYER *(to another girl)*

Let us wed in spring,
for it is written:
Marry in winter
while the chrysalis lives on its dreams,
and your dream will shatter
before spring comes.
But when it flies,
then God himself will open brooks and buds—

THIRD BRICKLAYER *(drinking thirstily)*

Always Israel was thirsty.
What people can ever have drunk at so many springs?
But now, thirst upon thirst,
all deserts together have worked at this our thirst.

A CARPENTER *with a door passes across the stage.* THE BEGGAR *with the feather in his hat enters*

BEGGAR

That is a door.
A door is a knife
and parts the world in two halves.
If I stand in front and knock on it
because I'm a beggar,
then perhaps it'll be opened to me

and the smell of roast meat
and the smell of soaked clothes stream out.
It is the smell of human homes.
He who has a fine beggar's nose
can smell tears too
or built-in well-being.
But the housewife says:
"No, it's too early in the day,"
and "No" says the closing door.
At the next door I come too late,
all I get is a glimpse
of a bed thrown open,
and the door shuts,
sad as an evening blessing.
Carpenter, hang no doors,
they are the knives
which cut the world apart.

CARPENTER

Man, collect your feather wits,
doors are for the cold and for burglars.
And since cold too is a burglar,
things are right as they are.

BEGGAR (*going up to the door and knocking*)

Here is Israel, door of the world,
Door of the world, open!

CARPENTER

It is well made,
it does not move,
but behind it,
the swallows migrate.

BEGGAR (*throwing himself on the sand before the door*)
There's your threshold!

TROOP OF YOUNG BRICKLAYERS
We build, we build
the new town, the new town,
the new town!
We bake, we bake
the bricks of the new town!

THE DAJAN
And Abraham raised his hovel
again and again
and set it in direction toward Him.

FIRST BRICKLAYER
Moses baked bricks,
David baked bricks,
now we bake bricks,
we the survivors!
His thornbush in the desert
are we, we, we!

SECOND BRICKLAYER
We bake!
and this here is our candle!

(*He stamps the earth with his foot*)

THIRD BRICKLAYER
We have new miracles!
Our desert too had quails and manna,
for a time I lived on snow,
ate clouds and sky—

Carpenter

What do you say to the secret of a potato peeling
washed up at my feet by the flood of hate?
That was my Ark.
If I now say "God,"
you know where the strength comes from.

Gardener *with an apple tree*

For a new Adam,
for a new Eve.

All (*singing*)

We bake, we bake,
to build the new house—

The Dajan

I fear you don't trench deep enough,
those foundations will only bear the easygoing.

(*Drinking at the fountain*)

The new Pentateuch, I tell you, the new Pentateuch
is written in mildew, the mildew of fear
on the walls of the death cellars.

First Bricklayer

Anguish of worms on the fishhook,
anguish of fish over the worm,
Anguish of beetles under my foot—
enough of the gravedigger's spade!

(*To* The Dajan)
Save your hay of memories for next winter—
here is fresh grass.

(*He wreathes a girl with grasses*)

Dust worshippers we are.
As long as the dust bears such fruit,
so long will we grub in its furrows
and make paradises of dust
with the apples
which like grim forebodings smell of departure—

GARDENER *with apple tree*

This comes from the alien earth.
The patriarchal dust is missing,
has nourished the holy citron—
Rachel of the well-deep eyes nourished it—
David, the shepherd of lambs.
My fingers crook themselves,
to sink its roots in alien earth—

FIRST BRICKLAYER

Perhaps the air will turn
into a new plant habitat,
in virtue of new inventions—
citron in the air,
home in the air.

ALL (*singing*)

We bake, we bake—

THE DAJAN (*to himself*)

I saw one who gnawed his own flesh
filling himself out to one side like the moon
and thinning down toward the other world—
I saw a child smile

before it was thrown on to the flames—
Where is that now?
My God, where is that now?

Curtain

Scene Ten

Country road. Uprooted or burned trees on either side. Fields churned up by warfare. Rank weeds flowering over them. Knife Grinder *and* Peddler Mendel *walking together, the latter with his stock on a handcart*

Knife Grinder (*pointing back along the road*)
They're all on edge a bit there, Brother Mendel.

Mendel
He who sits in the dark
lights himself a dream—
He who loses his bride
embraces the air—
He whose garment was touched by death
so that he cried out
has thoughts eating at him like worms—
A good thing I had hidden my stock
under the stonework.
Business wasn't bad today—

Knife Grinder
What did that man mean
when he picked out the one whose shoulder jerks
and you others?

Mendel

How should I know?
Once I saw a dowser,
his wand jumped up
whenever a spring was found.
So the Dajan seeks everywhere
the spring of hate
which was given Israel to drink.
But even though I knew better than I do,
you from another tribe,
how could I explain it to you?

Knife Grinder

Brother, why do you speak such words!
When we lay in the hayloft,
in the Pole Yarislav's hayloft,
then we were both one!
Eyes only, to espy the enemy,
ears only, to listen for creaking steps—
hair on the head
to rise to heaven in damp terror—
there came to us *one* sleep,
one hunger, *one* awakening,
came the yellow-eyed owl
who collects twigs
when she smells death—
looked into the loft window,
cried out like a hangman's daughter,
if he had had one:
Tuwoo!

Mendel

You made a gurgling sound in your dream
like a drowning man—

Knife Grinder

You spoke much about a light
that had set fire to your stock—

Mendel

Do you hear the crickets, Brother?

Knife Grinder

No.

Mendel

Pity.
It is the brightest sound in this world,
not every ear can catch it.
But did you see one?

Knife Grinder

No—

Mendel

Worse the pity.
They sit where the invisible begins.
They're beggars already at the gates of Paradise,
said Grandmother to us children.
But once a cricket was sitting
on a roll of rose-pink satin ribbon—

Knife Grinder (*to a stray dog which runs past*)

Here, here, comrade.
With your four paws
you can accompany my two.
If Mendel has his cricket,
I'll have my dog.
When I grind, he'll bark—

There'll be two for the wind to stroke,
two to hunger and stand outside,
with the earth under our paws.
When sun, moon, and stars enter his pupils—
and a whole world too.
O you warm, walking grain of earth
with two mirrors—

AN OLD BEGGAR MAN *comes to meet them*

MENDEL
Who are you, Grandpa?

OLD MAN
I am not nor am I Grandpa!

MENDEL
You are not, yet you speak!
Where do you come from?

OLD MAN (*pointing to the grinding wheel*)
Are you a knife grinder?

KNIFE GRINDER
Yes.

OLD MAN
So you know the truth.

KNIFE GRINDER
Why do you answer as in a question game?

OLD MAN
For the reason that there's fire in the stone,
and therefore life,

and in the knife death—
Therefore day by day you grind life with death.
That's where I come from.

KNIFE GRINDER
Alive out of death?

OLD MAN
From there where the murderers sowed my people in
the earth.
O may its seed be full of stars!

KNIFE GRINDER
By you?

OLD MAN
I was only half sown,
lying already in the grave,
knew already how the warmth leaves the flesh—
how motion leaves the bones—
heard already the language of the bones when
corruption sets in—
language of the blood when it congeals—
language of the dust
striving anew after love—

KNIFE GRINDER
But how were you saved?

MENDEL
Had you a ring,
a fine pearl to sell,
paid for your life with a secret glint?

OLD MAN

You wretched sacks,
stuffed with questions and quarreling.
What do you know of it,
when the bodies become empty
whispering like sea shells,
oh, when they rise on the white-flecked waves
of eternity?

KNIFE GRINDER

But tell us, how were you saved?

OLD MAN

We had fled,
Amschel, brown Yehudi, and I.
Three nations were taken captive
three languages taken captive,
hands taken captive
to be made to dig their own graves,
to grasp their own death.
Bodies were slaughtered
and the remains poured out on the ground.
How many thousands of millions of miles of anguish
from HIM!

MENDEL *and* KNIFE GRINDER

But you, you?

OLD MAN

The soldier
who filled in the earth over us
and buried us—
blessings be on him—
he saw by the lantern light,

for it was night,
that they had not slaughtered me enough
and that my eyes were opening—
and he fetched me out
and hid me—

KNIFE GRINDER
Very hard to believe.

MENDEL
There's no telling,
speak on.

OLD MAN
The soldier that morning—
so he told me later—
had had a letter from his mother.
Blessings be on her!
For that reason he was not intoxicated like the rest
and saw the blinking of my eyes.
The mother wrote:
"Really I meant to put this letter with the socks,
the home-knitted ones.
But my longing gave me no peace—"
blessings be on it!
"And I am writing today
without waiting till they are finished.
But your suit, the blue one,
has been brushed and hung out to air
because of the moth powder.
So it won't smell of it
when you come."
But it didn't happen

that she was able to post the letter at once,
for she fell ill during the night.
And a neighbor came—
blessings be on her!—
asked how she was—
but really all she wanted was an onion—
a small one to cook with her potatoes,
for her own were finished.
Ah, that she ate potatoes
and not turnips—
Blessed be all onions!—
and she was given an onion
and took the letter to the post
and the soldier got it on that morning
and did not get intoxicated like the others—
and saw the blinking of my eyes—

KNIFE GRINDER

How many onionskins came together there
to save you!
And what more will sprout
from your onion luck?

OLD MAN

I'm going to the Rabbi in the grave town.
My body will hold out no longer,
sand has touched the sand—
yet now it is the *one* death I die,
the other, which resides in a hangman's hand muscles
like a skeleton key in the burglar's fist,
that I don't need any more,
I have the right key!

KNIFE GRINDER *and* MENDEL *resume their walking*

MENDEL
I am pleased, I am pleased!

KNIFE GRINDER
What pleases you, Brother?

MENDEL
I am pleased
that I gave Michael a pair of laces
for his walking shoes.
If he reaches Paradise
he'll have my laces on his feet.
The death-shirt of Eli too was of my linen—

KNIFE GRINDER
Why was it good,
that you gave the shoemaker the laces,
and why should he die,
young as he is?

MENDEL (*as if telling him a secret*)
I don't know,
but good it is in any case.
He may be one of the Thirty-six
on whose deeds the world rests—
one who follows the course of the waters
and hears the turning of the earth—
one for whom the vein behind the ear
which for us throbs only in the hour of death
throbs every day,
one who wears Israel's walking shoes to the end—

KNIFE GRINDER (*to the dog*)

Here, then, come,
you look as if you were hungry.
The tongue hangs from your throat,
so you are thirsty too—
We'll go into the village,
if a twig of a stork's nest is still left of it,
to a farmer,
if a fingernail of a farmer's still to be found,
look for a sickle,
sharpen it
and cut with it the weeds in the field—
Perhaps we'll find a pool of water too,
in which death has not yet washed his bloody hands—
and then we'll drink—

(*He nods goodbye and walks across the field with the dog*)

MENDEL

Now it's as before.
Saved, but alone.

Curtain

SCENE ELEVEN

Night. A wood. An invisible light source illuminates
a fallen chimney and some trees with twisted branches.
MICHAEL *in his wandering stops and listens*

VOICE FROM THE CHIMNEY

We stones were the last things to touch Israel's sorrow.
Jeremiah's body in smoke,
Job's body in smoke,

the Lamentations in smoke,
whimpering of little children in smoke,
mothers' cradle songs in smoke,
Israel's way of freedom in smoke—

VOICE OF A STAR
I was the chimney sweep—
my light turned black—

TREE
I am a tree.
I can no longer stand straight.
It hung on me and swung
as though all the world's winds hung and swung
on me.

SECOND TREE
Blood pressed on to my roots—
All the birds which nested in my crown
had bloody nests.
Every evening I bleed afresh—
My roots climb from their grave—

FOOTPRINTS IN THE SAND
We filled the last minutes with death.
Grew ripe like apples from the heavy tread of men—
the mothers who touched us were in a hurry,
but the children were as light as spring rains—

VOICE OF THE NIGHT
Here are their last sighs,
I kept them for you,
feel them!
Their abode is in the never aging breezes—

in the breathing of those to come,
inconceivable in the sadness of night—

While MICHAEL *listens, there is seen, scarcely distinguishable from the tree roots,* A CREATURE *sitting on the ground, sewing at a white prayer shawl. Near him a death's head in the grass*

CREATURE

Michael!

MICHAEL (*approaching*)

Hirsch the tailor
in his lifetime looked like that.
You have perishable company with you—

CREATURE

Hirsch am I, the tailor, and my neighbor there
was someone's wife, perhaps my own—
I don't know—for although, there,

(*He points to the* CHIMNEY)

I was employed as Death,
once over the frontier it is hard to find anything again.
One minute past midnight
everything looks the same—
But however that may be,
if I'd listened to my blessed wife
I'd be sitting with the living in America,
among whom I have a brother—
not here among my like.
Look, she said
when it all began,
You're a stag, Hirsch, a stag,

so you must scent it coming
or hasn't the Jewish people
a nose for what's in store?—
the knives are stirring in the drawer,
the scissors of the great tailor are grating,
and the fire in the stove is forming grisly faces
as in the Witch of Endor's cave—
But above all, I feel glances,
glances squinting like the cat's—
Michael, Michael—
you they have not touched,
you they have spared,
and you stood up to them everywhere,
so to speak to windward,
as my one-time customer, the gamekeeper, would
  have said,
like a game animal
which has lost its scent—
but me they brought to bay
because of my protruding cheekbones
and also because of my legs.
Death, you have two sickle blades,
they said,
it's quicker that way.
Unless you send your people up in smoke,
unless you burn your own flesh and blood
we'll unscrew your pelvis
and remove your two sickle blades.
And then you'll have better food
than all of us together.
Smoke weighs more heavily in the stomach than
  bread—

(He lays the prayer shawl aside. Pointing to the death's head)

It is too dark, that one there
doesn't shine any more—
And I burned them
and I ate smoke,
and I stoked HIM into the fire.
And I ran into the wood
and there stood raspberry canes,
and I ate raspberries
after I had stoked HIM into the fire,
and I could not die,
because I am Death
but look there—

(Shouting)
look there—

CHIMNEY

I am the Camp Commandant.
March, march
go the thoughts out of my head!

Smoke begins to rise and transform itself into transparent shapes. Moon and stars shed a black light. The tree roots are corpses with twisted limbs. THE CREATURE *gets up and throws the prayer shawl high into the smoke*

A GIANT FORM *wraps itself in it and rises singing into the sky*

Hear, O Israel.
He our God,
He the One—

THE CHIMNEY *crumbles*

THE CREATURE *is struck, dying*

Hear, O Israel
He our God,
He the One—

FOOTPRINTS IN THE SAND

Come gathering, gathering, Michael,
a time is there again,
a time which had run out—
gather it up—
gather it up—

MICHAEL *stoops, walking in the footprints*

MICHAEL

He who goes gathering death moments
needs not a basket, but a heart to fill—

Curtain

SCENE TWELVE

Frontier of the neighboring country. Heath and moorland

MICHAEL

All signposts point downward.
Foxgloves grow here—
no, not gloves but fingers
grow here like weeds,
not like those flowers
with which Miriam filled her little shoe

when she broke the strap:
"The gloved fingers will stroke you," she said,
"as you sew it up."
The fingers which grow here
are fingers of men's hands.

VOICES OF THE FINGERS

We are the fingers of the killers.
Each one wears a premeditated death
like a false moonstone.
Look, Michael, like this—

A FINGER (*reaching for* MICHAEL'S *throat*)

My finger's speciality was strangling,
the compression of the windpipe
with a slight turn to the right.

(*Gurgling noise*)

MICHAEL *has sunk to the ground*

VOICE OF THE SECOND KILLER

Your knees, Michael,
your wrists—
do you hear, of glass—
everything is fragile on earth.
A good man's not afraid of dust,
and here's a wineglassful of blood—

MICHAEL

Great death, great death, come—

VOICE OF THE SECOND KILLER

That's out of fashion.
Here are the small dainty deaths—
your neck—
just there where the hair gets downy—

Voice of the Third Killer

In the name of Science—
this injection—
Whoever volunteers turns light-colored
like rotten wood—

Long Bony Finger

Don't be afraid.
I want neither to bid good night to your windpipe
nor to be rough to your joints.
I'm only the professorial finger
of the new wisdom.
I want a little conversation with your gray matter—

Michael

Away—

Voice of the Professorial Finger

Job is grown weak,
tired organ-grinder of a once-fresh tune.
The seas have been drawn out into horsepower
  on one hand
and into tap water on the other.
Their ebb and flow are in the hands of a
  moon-man.
Michael the shoemaker
sews sole and uppers together
with his waste-product thread—
Shoemaker saint!
Were the fountain pens asleep among you
which should have bought your people free?

Voice of the Wildly Gesticulating Finger

I am the conductor's finger.
I conducted the music for their good night.

March music is heard
Old the world had to become
before the hate
which bloodily sought
to solve the Jew puzzle
hit on the notion
of banishing it from the world with music—

The music becomes weaker. THE FINGERS, *held by a giant finger on strings, dance their respective activities.* THE PROFESSORIAL FINGER *taps* MICHAEL *on the head. The Earth falls like a black apple*

MICHAEL (*shouting*)
Is that star lost?

ECHO
Lost!

MICHAEL'S VOICE
Hear me . . .

Curtain

SCENE THIRTEEN

Open field. MICHAEL *lying on the ground, gets up.* A FARMER *with a cow on a halter approaches*

MICHAEL
The fingers last pointed in this direction,
murderers betray the murderer in the end.
How peaceful in daylight this spot looks.
The crickets sing,

a jay calls its mate.
The cow has the primeval face
of a creature just stroked by its Creator's hand.
As everywhere, the farmer is tasting out the
secret of the wheat grain.

(*To the* FARMER)
A good evening to you,
would there be a shoemaker's in this
neighborhood?

FARMER
You come from over there, across the frontier?
You've death on your brow—

MICHAEL
How can you tell?

FARMER
When a man has something shining between
the eyes,
big as a snowflake—

MICHAEL
May be
that the death of my people shines in me.

FARMER
A Pole are you or even—a Jew?

MICHAEL
On this earth I am both.

Farmer

That is much!
There beyond the big meadow
is the way to the village.
Next door to the inn garden
is the shoemaker's shop.

A Child *has joined them.* Michael *pulls out his shepherd's pipe and plays*

Child

If I'd a pipe like that
I'd be piping day and night,
I'd be piping in my sleep—

Michael

It's from a dead child—

Farmer (*repeating*)

From a dead child—

Michael

From a boy
who was murdered—

Farmer

Who was murdered—

Michael

As his parents were being driven to their death
he ran after in his shirt—

Farmer

After in his shirt—

MICHAEL

On this pipe he piped to God for help—

FARMER

Piped to God for help—

MICHAEL

Then a soldier struck him dead—

FARMER

Then a soldier struck him dead—

MICHAEL *plays his pipe. Children, calves, sheep, and foals come frisking to it.* THE MOTHERS *lift up their babies. Some* MEN, *sickle in hand, lower their heads*

Curtain

SCENE FOURTEEN

House of the village schoolteacher. In the garden stand the SCHOOLTEACHER *and his* SON *looking up into the great linden tree.* BOYS *are practicing stone-throwing at a scarecrow, made of old bits of war gear and metal parts, in the plowed field*

BOY (*after throwing*)

That sounded as if someone had cried out.

CHILD

Yes, it was Isidor the peddler's voice
as we drove him out of the village.
Oy, he said, oy,
and there he lay in the ditch.

Boy

And reached out for his cap,
look, like this, with his hand turned inward,
just as he used to do when weighing things—
and Hans called out:
"Has the evening sun caught your cap?"
and gave him another to remember us by—

Schoolteacher

There hangs the bee swarm.
Hark to the music it makes.
There'll be honey,
never has the linden tree flowered so well,
what luck
that it was spared by men's wars.

Boy

How nice it smells here, Father, O!
And then the honey on our bread, O!

Mother (*from the house*)

I'll just pick the lettuce
and chop the chervil for the soup,
dinner will soon be ready.
Why don't you get out your butterfly net, Hans?
Look at all those moths on the thyme—

Boy (*picking up a stone*)

Just a minute!

Schoolteacher

Leave the scarecrow alone,
too much corpse smell in the field,
the crows get more and more—

BOY (*pointing at* MICHAEL)
No, there I'll throw it.

SCHOOLTEACHER
Don't do that!

BOY
Why yesterday and not today?

SCHOOLTEACHER
Although I teach arithmetic,
that's a mathematical puzzle I can't solve—

MICHAEL *walks past*

BOY (*to himself*)
Yesterday I'd have sent the stone after him,
it'd have fallen near the manure pit, I expect,
after first tripping two feet.
Today it stays in my hand,
but I'll throw it into the pond,
to give something a fright at least—

Curtain

SCENE FIFTEEN

Shoemaker's shop in frontier village

SHOEMAKER
No, not like that, no truly!
Only—perhaps you are for us
like shoes of former times, of long ago.

They fitted nobody,
good leather, but unsuited—
not for our climate,
for the deserts perhaps,
for the Holy Land perhaps,
for those markets perhaps
where the Isidors hawk their wares differently
  from us—
but of course as things went with you then—
no, that we didn't want—
not like that—

MICHAEL

Since Abraham wandered forth from Ur
we have spent our efforts
to build our house toward HIM
as others build facing the sun—
True, many turned themselves in the opposite
  direction—
Old shepherds let the star clocks strike unheeded
and slept like Isidor the pawnbroker with
  crooked fingers—
But there was a boy—
Master, the sole cries out in my hand,
it reeks of death—

SHOEMAKER

May be so,
for a dying steer stretched out its paws
and then—

A MAN *enters, holding a small child by the hand*

Are my shoes ready?

Shoemaker

My assistant's just working on them—

Michael

This sole can't be patched,
it's torn up the middle.

Man

Make me a new sole then—

Child

Father, this is the man
who had the pipe.
There it is on the flowerpot.
O let me play it!

Man

You don't play strangers' pipes.

Child (*crying*)

The pipe—

Man

She's crying
because she wants her mother.
She always wants something:
One day it's the blackbird
which used to come for scraps
and disappeared,
another it's the old sheepdog
which ran across the rails
and was run over—

MICHAEL (*aloud*)

Everything begins with wanting.
Even this here—

(*He lets earth from the flowerpot trickle through his hands*)

And these here—

(*He points to the hides from which the shoes are cut*)

CHILD

The pipe—

MAN

I'll buy you a pipe.
When you've got it,
all the children will follow you
and give you their toys—

CHILD

No, *this* pipe,
then the cows'll come and the little calves.

THE MAN *takes the child by the hand, and as they go out*

SHOEMAKER'S WIFE (*at the door*)

I want something too.
Farmer, when'll you have a roast to spare?
With me it's the mouth
that does the wanting.
What kind of want is that?

Curtain

SCENE SIXTEEN
A farmhouse bedroom

CHILD *asleep*

MAN

Teeth everywhere,
do you hear how it rattles?
Hollow tooth where oats should be.
Black horse climbing,
shaking its mane,
and showing its teeth.
The calves drink with their teeth
and fleck the udders with blood—
the rye-stalks bitten off—teeth without rats—
Do you hear it, Wife,
here in the room,
there, there!

(*She points to the wall*)

Teeth where bricks should be—
Wife, the bricklayer must to the gallows—

WIFE

Be quiet now,
the child's asleep,
the fever's very high!

MAN

Now it's rattling,
the whole house rattles—

(*His teeth chatter*)

CHILD (*in a dream*)
All the trees go walking
all the trees go walking
lift up their root-feet and walk
when I pipe—

MAN (*singing*)
All the shades go walking,
come, dear hearse-cloth,
cover up the white moon-tooth for me.
Wasn't it a milk-tooth
which dropped from his mouth with the pipe—
Wife, wife,
the milk has teeth,
teeth—

A knock on the window

MAN (*opening the window*)
Who's there?

BAKER
Baker Hans.
Here's a sugar pretzel for little Annie.
The iron pretzel,
my good shop-sign from the Jew baker in Poland,
has turned red.
They're whispering already.
The dead children don't touch the pretzel crumbs
I scatter for them into the night,
and drag the malt away.
Lately they sat like a swarm of wasps

on the shop counter.
The squint-eyed child stamped its feet on the wood,
as if to warm itself,
then it climbed bolt upright to the ceiling
and hung there like flypaper.
In the morning it fell off.
The flies had eaten it up.

MAN (*rattling the windowpane, which is lit up by the moon*)
Look, that's how you did with the squint-
eyed one—
Here's the pretzel,
there's the pretzel,
till it had ceased to squint.
Now it's squinting your day away,
as mine is chewed by the milk-tooth.

BAKER
They say
you once killed a holy child?

MAN
Stuff and nonsense!
All children are holy.

POSTMAN (*coming on*)
Why do you quarrel for first place in child
murder?

BAKER
Sorter of cry-baby parcels!
Did no sender
write "Fragile" on them?

Postman

My orders were
to heed the addressee,
not the sender.

Doctor *(coming out of the bedroom)*

Your child—

Wife *(coming on)*

The child is dead!

Curtain

Scene Seventeen

Country road. On either side, thick pine forest. Michael *walking. Behind a pine tree,* The Man *is standing*

Michael

A look has pierced my back,
I am held fast.

They look at one another

Man

If he hadn't thrown his head back
I shouldn't have struck him down,
the milk-tooth wouldn't have fallen out with
the pipe.
But—that was contrary to Order—
to throw the head back—
that had to be corrected.

And where did he pipe to?
A secret signal?
A signal through the air—
beyond all control—
Help, shoemaker,
the milk-tooth is growing out of the earth—
beginning to gnaw at me—
right through my shoe—
my feet are crumbling—
becoming earth—

(*Shrieking*)

Where's the Order in all this, the World Order—
I am alive,
I am not dead—
not hung—
not burned—
not thrown live into the earth— —

(*At the top of his voice*)
It's a mistake, a mistake,
I'm crumbling, crumbling—
I'm a stump—
sitting on the sand
that a moment ago was my flesh—

The air has opened out into circles. In the first circle appears THE EMBRYO *in its mother's womb, with the primal light on its brow*

VOICE

Child with the light of God,
read in the hands of the murderer—

MAN

My hands, my hands—
don't leave me, O my hands—

(His hands crumble off)

The horizon opens out as the greatest of the circles.
A BLEEDING MOUTH *appears like a setting sun*

VOICE

Open,
dumb mouth of Samuel!

VOICE OF SAMUEL

Eli!

The mother's womb dissolves in smoke. The primal light fastens on to MICHAEL's *brow*

MICHAEL

Crumbling one!
His eyes become holes—
the light seeks out other mirrors.
I see through the holes—
glasses for the sun's eclipse—
into your skull
which frames that world
which you as commanded have packed inside it,
as in a soldier's knapsack—
There it lies—twitching,
an insect star with wings torn off—
In it stirs a hand
that stole a lightning bolt—
A raven consumes a human leg—

lightning consumes the raven—
I see nothing more—

VOICE

Footprints of Israel,
gather yourselves together!
Last earthly moments of Israel,
gather yourselves together!
Last moments of suffering,
gather yourselves together!

MICHAEL

Under my feet it jumps up.
From my hands it plunges down.
My heart pours something out—

VOICE

Your shoes are worn to pieces—come!

MICHAEL *is gathered up and vanishes*

Final Curtain

Postscript to ELI

This mystery play has as its leading figure Michael, a young shoemaker. In Hassidic mysticism he is one of the secret Servants of God who, thirty-six in number (and quite unaware of it themselves), carry the invisible universe. According to the prophet Isaiah, the Lord puts the arrow he has used back in its quiver so that it may remain in darkness. Thus Michael feels, darkly, the inner call to seek the murderer of the child Eli, the child who raised to heaven the shepherd's pipe with which he used to call the cattle together—"like the stag or roebuck before it drinks at the spring"—to pipe to God, as his parents were being taken away to their death. A young soldier, believing this to be a secret signal (symbol of unbelief), struck the boy dead.

Michael goes his quiet way through this legend made of truth, sees in the shadow thrown by a light on Eli's death shirt the face of the murderer, and in transcendental fashion experiences once more during his travels the bloody events of our forsaken age. The murderer, when Michael finally sees him face to face, crumbles to dust before the divine light shining from Michael's countenance (picture of remorse).

In this world of night, where a secret equilibrium seems to reign, the victim is always innocence. The child Eli and the child of the murderer both die, victims of evil.

This mystery play was the outcome of a terrible experience of the Hitler time at the height of its smoke and flame, and was written down in a few nights after my flight to Sweden.

The shepherd's pipe raised in desperation by a child to God—attempted outbreak of the human in the face of horror.

The soldier: "If he hadn't thrown his head back, I shouldn't have struck him down . . ."

That was a sign beyond all control—could be a secret signal.

No more trust in good on earth.

Written in a rhythm which must make the Hassidic mystical fervor visible also in mime to the performer—the encounter with the divine radiance which accompanies each of our everyday words. Always designed to raise the unutterable to a transcendental level, so as to make it bearable and in this night of nights to give a hint of the holy darkness in which quiver and arrow are hidden.